SAVOIR

• • • • • • •

THE HUMORISTS GUIDE TO FRANCE

Other Humorists' Guides

When in Rome: The Humorists' Guide to Italy
All in the Same Boat: The Humorists' Guide
to the Ocean Cruise

SAVOIR RIRE

· · · · · · · · · · · · · ·

THE HUMORISTS' GUIDE to FRANCE

Edited by Robert Wechsler

 Robson Books

First published in Great Britain in 1989 by Robson Books Ltd,
Bolsover House, 5–6 Clipstone Street, London W1P 7EB

British Library Cataloguing in Publication Data

Savoir rire: the humorists' guide to France.
  1. France. Description & travel, 1643-1715
  I. Wechsler, Robert, 1954–
  914.4'04838

ISBN 0 86051 575 3

Printed in Great Britain by
Billing & Sons Ltd., Worcester

CONTENTS

INTRODUCTION

TRAVEL guides are what you read when you want to know where to stay and what to see and where to eat and what to do about such things as visas and hotels and shopping. This is not that sort of guide.

Humorists don't keep track of price fluctuations; they go on and on about that institution called tipping, or *pourboire* if you will, which is what the humorists are sure it's all for: "for drinking." Humorists are sure that wherever you stay there'll be a concierge at the door who soon knows everything about you, and a pacing patriot upstairs who will not be parted from his boots until midnight rings out on all the mistimed bell towers in all those lovely churches you came to see.

So forget everything you've ever thought about guidebooks. The advice here is much simpler: relax and enjoy. Remember, it's your vacation — holiday time — so don't annoy yourself about the prices or the services or the cabbies. Well, if you have to worry about something, go ahead and worry about the cabbies; but it won't do you any good.

Although we go to France to see the Rodins and Manets, what we see more of, and what humorists can never get enough of, are the Augustes and Edouards, not to mention the Maries and Michelles and our fellow Johns and Marys. Humor is about people, about how they react to all those things the travel guides describe, as well as how they react to each other. Humor couldn't care less about *what* will serve us best; it prefers to look at *who* will manage not to. It is interested not in where we set down our bags, but in the baggage we carry with us: awe and delight, playfulness and absurdity, dreams and nightmares, myths and stereotypes, platitudes and pretensions, expectations and obsessions, anger and fear and love. And no trip is complete without Us and Them.

France. The word conjures up more than a second-rate magician. We sigh at the sound (and sight) of its tongue: Rive Gauche, Riviera, Catherine Deneuve. We adore the Impressionists, Post-Impressionists, Cubists, and all the other wonderful schools the French have managed to come up with. And nothing is romantic as Paris. In other words, France is a sitting duck for humor.

Think of it. How can anyone help laughing at a country that thinks Jerry Lewis is the funniest man since Charlemagne's fool, and worse still, has the *gall* to take itself seriously? What could be more ridiculous!

Yes, *Savoir Rire* is more than just another pretty guidebook. Behind that sparkling veneer is a serious humor anthology. Among the selections are many that are simply fun or silly or non-sensical, many that make unusual or ironic observations, many that satire or parody or find some other way to poke fun at, many that take delight in what they see, for better or for worse, and some that do all of these at once. Although many of the selections are vintage, the humor here is not about the way things used to be; it's too easy to laugh at our fathers and grandmothers. This is a book about the way things still are and will, most likely, be.

There are unknown finds in *Savoir Rire*, such as Melville Chater's "A Heathen Father's Fable," as well as classics of the genre, such as Mark Twain's "Climbing Mont Blanc." There is even one great piece of poetry, which is made humorous primarily because it is spoken by a cockroach: Don Marquis' "archy at the tomb of napoleon" (you see, poor archy couldn't hold down the shift key).

Many of the greatest English-speaking humorists and cartoonists are represented in these pages, some of them long out-of-print, but not forgotten. Britons will recognize the names of Max Beerbohm, Laurence Sterne, Owen Seaman, and Alan Coren. Americans will recognize the names of James Thurber, Art Buchwald, Ring Lardner, Robert Benchley, Will Rogers, S. J. Perelman, and Mark Twain, who did not invent, but certainly popularized the humorous travelogue way back in 1869. And all Canadians will know the name of Stephen Leacock. But less well known today everywhere are such excellent humorists as, chronologically, Petroleum V. Nasby (David R. Locke), Bill Nye, Irvin S. Cobb, Don Marquis, Homer Croy, Alexander Woollcott, Christopher Morley, Frank Sullivan, Donald Moffat, Donald Ogden Stewart, Margaret Fishback, A. J. Liebling, and Emily Kimbrough.

Savoir Rire also includes selections from the work of travel writers with a sense of humor, many of whom are well known from their other works, mostly novels. People like Charles Dickens, Theodore Dreiser, Hart Crane, Heywood Broun, Ford Madox Ford, and Ludwig Bemelmans. There are also a number of travel writers not so well remembered, but certainly deserving of space.

And we can't forget the cartoonists and illustrators. Few of them are household names; in fact, that honor goes to Mark Twain, whose illustration to the section on Paris may be his only one in print (you'll see why). But few humorists or humor magazines would be the same without them: Gluyas Williams, Robert Benchley's alter ego; Al Hirschfeld, S. J. Perelman's graphic man and caricaturist extraordinaire; Herb Roth, who graced the work of Donald Ogden Stewart and others; Laszlo Matulay, who let us in on what Art Buchwald looked like in France and what France looked like to Art Buchwald; and just a few of the cartoonists who have made *Punch* a national institution on a par with Princess Di (well, maybe a bogey): Geoffrey Dickinson, Haldane, Walter Goetz, and Sally Artz.

Well, that's enough names. At least now you won't have to bother with the table of contents. Enjoy, and let me thank all the people who helped make *Savoir Rire* possible, particularly the all-too-forgotten souls (are they humorists?!) who work in the permissions departments of publishing houses; the families of the humorists; the literary agents; and, most of all, those humorists who have begrudgingly stuck around to force upon us more of their fun. Special thanks go to Mircea Vasiliu, whose work graces the cover and who brought to delightful life all the wanderings of Emily Kimbrough; and to Len Ringel, who designed everything you're looking at.

"Three billion light years just to try out his French."

❧Preparations

❧ *The first thing we do when we decide to go somewhere is to run out and buy a travel guide or two, to help us decide where to go (Brittany? No, too cold. The Riviera? No, all you'll do is stare. The Loire? Everyone does it.) and what sort of place to stay in (A* pension? *Too dirty. A* château? *Too expensive. A* hotel? *In* France?!). *The more ambitious of us decide to buy a French phrasebook and bone up at least on what we'll need to know to win an argument with our con-cierge. We've never gotten past the pronunciation section before and, on the plane perhaps, please and thank you. But this time . . . Well, after reading what James Thurber has to say about the apparently innocent phrasebook, you might feel relieved you've gotten no further.*

James Thurber
There's No Place Like Home 1940

IDLING through a London bookstore in the summer of 1937, I came upon a little book called "Collins' Pocket Interpreters: France." Written especially to instruct the English how to speak French in the train, the hotel, the quandary, the dilemma, etc., it is, of course, equally useful — I might also say equally depressing — to Ameri-cans. I have come across a number of these helps-for-travelers, but none that has the heavy impact, the dark, cumulative power of Col-lins'. A writer in a London magazine mentions a phrase book got out in the era of Imperial Russia which contained this one magnificent line: "Oh, dear, our postillion has been struck by lightning!" but the fantastic piece of disaster, while charming and provocative — though, I daresay, quite rare even in the days of the Czars — is to Mr. Collins' modern, workaday disasters as Fragonard is to George Bel-lows, or Sarah Orne Jewett to William Faulkner. Let us turn the pages of this appalling little volume.

Each page has a list of English expressions one under the other, which gives them the form of verse. The French translations are run alongside. Thus, on the first page, under "The Port of Arrival," we begin (quietly enough) with "Porter, here is my baggage!" — *"Porteur, voici mes bagages!"* From then on disaster follows fast and follows faster until in the end, as you shall see, all hell breaks loose. The volume contains three times as many expressions to use when one is in trouble as when everything is going all right. This, my own experience has shown, is about the right ratio, but God spare me from some of the difficulties for which the traveler is prepared in Mr. Collins' melancholy narrative poem. I am going to leave out the French translations because, for one thing, people who get involved in the messes and tangles we are coming to invariably forget their French and scream in English anyway. Furthermore, the French would interrupt the fine, free flow of the English and spoil what amounts to a dramatic tragedy of an overwhelming and original kind. The phrases, as I have said, run one under the other, but herein I shall have to run them one after the other (you can copy them down the other way, if you want to).

Trouble really starts in the canto called "In the Customs Shed." Here we have: "I cannot open my case." "I have lost my keys." "Help me to close this case." "I did not know that I had to pay." "I don't want to pay so much." "I cannot find my porter." "Have you seen porter 153?" That last query is a little master stroke of writing, I think, for in those few words we have a graphic picture of a tourist lost in a jumble of thousands of bags and scores of customs men, looking frantically for one of at least a hundred and fifty-three porters. We feel that the tourist will not find porter 153, and the note of frustration has been struck.

Our tourist (accompanied by his wife, I like to think) finally gets on the train for Paris — having lost his keys and not having found his porter — and it comes time presently to go to the dining car, although he probably has no appetite, for the customs men, of course, had to break open that one suitcase. Now, I think, it is the wife who begins to crumble: "Someone has taken my seat." "Excuse me, sir, that seat is mine." "I cannot find my ticket!" "I have left my ticket in the compartment." "I will go and look for it." "I have left my gloves (my purse) in the dining car." Here the note of frenzied disintegration, so familiar to all travelers abroad, is sounded. Next comes "The Sleeper," which begins, ominously, with "What is the matter?" and ends with "May I open the window?" "Can you open this window, please?" We realize, of course, that *nobody* is going to be able to open the window and that the tourist and his wife will suffocate. In this condition they arrive in Paris, and the scene there, on the crowded station platform, is done with superb economy of line: "I have left something in the train." "A parcel, an overcoat." "A mackintosh, a stick." "An umbrella, a camera." "A fur, a suitcase." The travelers have now begun to go completely to pieces, in the grand manner.

Next comes an effective little interlude about an airplane trip, which is one of my favorite passages in this swift and sorrowful tragedy: "I want to reserve a place in the plane leaving tomorrow morning." "When do we start?" "Can we get anything to eat on board?" "When do we arrive?" "I feel sick." "Have you any paper bags for airsickness?" "The noise is terrible." "Have you any cotton wool?" "When are we going to land?" This brief master-piece caused me to cancel an air trip from London to Paris and go the easy way, across the Channel.

We now come to a section called "At the Hotel," in which things go from worse to awful: "Did you not get my letter?" "I wrote to you three weeks ago." "I asked for a first-floor room." "If you can't give me something better, I shall go away." "The chambermaid never comes when I ring." "I cannot sleep at night, there is so much noise." "I have just had a wire. I must leave at once." Panic has begun to set in, and it is not appeased any by the advent of "The Chambermaid": "Are you the chambermaid?" "There are no towels here." "The sheets on this bed are damp." "This room is not clean." "I have seen a mouse in the room." "You will have to set a mouse trap here." The bells of hell at this point begin to ring in earnest: "These shoes are not mine." "I put my shoes here, where are they now?" "The light is not good." "The bulb is broken." "The radiator is too warm." "The radiator doesn't work." "It is cold in this room." "This is not clean, bring me another." "I don't like this." "I can't eat this. Take it away!"

I somehow now see the tourist's wife stalking angrily out of the hotel, to get away from it all (without any shoes on), and, properly enough, the booklet seems to follow her course — first under "Guides and Interpreters": "You are asking too much." "I will not give you any more." "I shall call a policeman." "He can settle this affair." Then under "Inquiring the Way": "I am lost." "I was looking for —" "Someone robbed me." "That man robbed me." "That man is following me everywhere." She rushes to "The Hairdresser," where, for a change, everything goes quite smoothly until: "The water is too hot, you are scalding me!" Then she goes shopping, but there is no surcease: "You have not given me the right change." "I bought this two days ago." "It doesn't work." "It is broken." "It is torn." "It doesn't fit me." Then to a restaurant for a snack and a reviving cup of tea: "This is not fresh." "This piece is too fat." "This doesn't smell very nice." "There is a mistake in the bill." "While I was dining someone has taken my purse." "I have left my glasses (my watch) (a ring) in the lavatory." Madness has now come upon her and she rushes wildly out into the street. Her husband, I think, has at the same time plunged blindly out of the hotel to find her. We come then, quite naturally, to "Accident," which is calculated to keep the faint of heart — nay, the heart of oak — safely at home by his own fireside: "There has been an accident!" "Go and fetch a policeman quickly." "Is there a doctor near here?" "Send for the ambulance." "He is seriously injured." "She has been run over." "He has been knocked down." "Someone has fallen in the water." "The ankle, the arm." "The back, a bone." "The face, the finger." "The foot, the head." "The knee, the leg." "The neck, the nose." "The wrist, the shoulder." "He has broken his arm." "He has a sprained wrist." "He is losing blood." "He has broken his leg." "He has a sprained ankle." "He has fainted." "He has lost consciousness." "He has burnt his face." "It is swollen." "It is bleeding." "Bring some cold water." "Help me to carry him." (Apparently, you just let *her* lie there, while you attend to him — but, of course, she was merely run over, whereas he has taken a terrific tossing around.)

We next see the husband and wife back in their room at the dreary hotel, both in bed, and both obviously hysterical. This scene is entitled "Illness": "I am feeling very ill, send for the doctor." "I have pains in —" "I have pains all over." "The back, the chest." "The ear, the head." "The eyes, the heart." "The joints, the kidneys." "The lungs, the stomach." "The throat, the tongue." "Put our your tongue." "The heart is affected." "I feel a pain here." "He is not sleeping well." "He cannot eat." "My stomach is out of order." "She is feverish." "I have caught a cold." "I have caught a chill." "He has a temperature." "I have a cough." "Will you give me a prescription?" "What must I do?" "Must I stay in bed?" "I feel better." "When will you come and see me again?" "Biliousness, rheumatism." "Insomnia, sunstroke." "Fainting, a fit." "Hoarseness, sore throat." "The medicine, the remedy." "A poultice, a draught." "A tablespoonful, a teaspoonful." "A sticking plaster, senna." "Iodine." That last suicidal bleat for iodine is, to me, a masterful touch.

Our couple finally get on their feet again, for travelers are tough — they've got to be — but we see under the next heading, "Common Words and Phrases," that they are left forever punch-drunk and shattered: "Can I help you?" "Excuse me." "Carry on!" "Look here!" "Look down there!" "Look up there!" "Why, how?" "When, where?" "Because." "That's it!" "It is too much, it is too dear." "It is very cheap." "Who, what, which?" "Look out!" Those are Valkyries, one feels, riding around, and above, and under our unhappy husband and wife. The book sweeps on to a mad operatic ending of the tragedy, with all the strings and brasses and wood winds going full blast: "Where are we going?" "Where are you going?" "Come quickly and see!" "I shall call a policeman." "Bring a policeman!" "I shall stay here." "Will you help me?" "Help! Fire!" "Who are you?" "I don't know you." "I don't want to speak to you." "Leave me alone." "That will do." "You are mistaken." "It was not I." "I didn't do it." "I will give you nothing." "Go away now!" "It has nothing to do with me." "Where should one apply?" "What must I do?" "What have I done?" "I have done nothing." "I have already paid you." "I have paid you enough." "Let me pass!" "Where is the British consulate?" The oboes take that last, despairing wail, and the curtain comes down.

Of course, the best introduction to the French language or, as they say, tongue, as well as to the suave Frenchman or the luscious French-woman, is to study French in a class or, better yet, with a tutor. There, through one level or another of linguistic and cultural immersion, you will feel initiated before you even take off.

Theodore Tilton
French with a Master 1900

Teach you French? I will, my dear!
Sit and con your lesson here.
What did Adam say to Eve?
Aimer, aimer; c'est à vivre.

Don't pronounce the last word long;
Make it short to suit the song;
Rhyme it to your flowing sleeve,
Aimer, aimer; c'est à vivre.

Sleeve, I said, but what's the harm
If I really meant your arm?
Mine shall twine it (by your leave),
Aimer, aimer; c'est à vivre.

Learning French is full of slips;
Do as I do with the lips;
Here's the right way, you perceive,
Aimer, aimer; c'est à vivre.

French is always spoken best
Breathing deeply from the chest;
Darling, does your bosom heave?
Aimer, aimer; c'est à vivre.

Now, my dainty little sprite,
Have I taught your lesson right?
Then what pay shall I receive?
Aimer, aimer; c'est à vivre.

Pretty pupil, when you say
All this French to me to-day,
Do you mean it, or deceive?
Aimer, aimer; c'est à vivre.

Tell me, may I understand,
When I press your little hand,
That our hearts together cleave?
Aimer, aimer; c'est à vivre.

Or, if I presume too much
Teaching French by sense of touch,
Grant me pardon and reprieve!
Aimer, aimer; c'est à vivre.

Sweetheart, no! you cannot go!
Let me sit and hold you so;
Adam did the same to Eve, —
Aimer, aimer; c'est à vivre.

Incomprehensible Jargon

*A*fter dinner we felt like seeing such Parisian specialties as we might see without distressing exertion, and so we sauntered through the brilliant streets and looked at the dainty trifles in variety stores and jewelry shops. Occasionally, merely for the pleasure of being cruel, we put unoffending Frenchmen on the rack with questions framed in the incomprehensible jargon of their native language, and while they writhed, we impaled them, we peppered them, we scarified them, with their own vile verbs and participles. — *Mark Twain, 1869*

PARIS IN THE NOSE

✑Arrival

✑France never seems real at first; it's hard to believe one's entered the mythically over-historied land of Louises, Napoleons, and de Gaulle (there's only one, so far). Of course, arrival by plane is the same in every metropolis, but arriving by boat, especially by ferry across the Channel, or La Manche, is something very special. Hurry up and go before they build the Chunnel and no one will know what it's like to love and hate Calais the way Charles Dickens did.

Charles Dickens
The Calais Night Mail 1860

IT is an unsettled question with me whether I shall leave Calais something handsome in my will, or whether I shall leave it my malediction. I hate it so much, and yet I am always so very glad to see it, that I am in a state of constant indecision on this subject.

When I first made acquaintance with Calais, it was as a maundering young wretch in a clammy perspiration and dripping saline particles, who was conscious of no extremities but the one great extremity, sea-sickness, — who was a mere bilious torso, with a mislaid headache somewhere in its stomach, — who had been put into a horrible swing in Dover Harbour, and had tumbled giddily out of it on the French coast, or the Isle of Man, or anywhere. Times have changed, and now I enter Calais self-reliant and rational. I know where it is beforehand, I keep a lookout for it, I recognise its landmarks when I see any of them, I am acquainted with its ways, and I know — and I can bear — its worst behaviour.

Malignant Calais! Low-lying alligator, evading the eyesight and discouraging hope! Dodging flat streak, now on this bow, now on that, now anywhere, now everywhere, now nowhere! In vain Cape Grinez, coming frankly forth into the sea, exhorts the failing to be stout of heart and stomach; sneaking Calais, prone behind its bar, invites emetically to despair. Even when it can no longer quite conceal itself in its muddy dock, it has an evil way of falling off, has Calais, which is more hopeless than its invisibility. The pier is all but on the bowsprit, and you think you are there — roll, roar, wash! — Calais has retired miles inland, and Dover has burst out to look for it. It has a last dip and slide in its character, has Calais, to be especially commended to the infernal gods. Thrice accursed be that garrison town, when it dives under the boat's keel, and comes up a league or two to the right, with the packet shivering and sputtering and staring about for it!

A stout wooden wedge driven in at my right temple and out at my left, a floating deposit of lukewarm oil in my throat, and a compression of the bridge of my nose in a blunt pair of pincers, — these are the personal sensations by which I know we are off, and by which I shall continue to know it until I am on the soil of France. My symptoms have scarcely established themselves comfortably, when two or three skating shadows that have been trying to walk or stand get flung together, and other two or three shadows in tarpaulin slide with them into corners and cover them up. Then the South Foreland lights begin to hiccup at us in a way that bodes no good.

It is at about this period that my detestation of Calais knows no bounds. Inwardly, I resolve afresh that I never will forgive that hated town. I have done so before, many times; but that is past. Let me register a vow. Implacable animosity to Calais everm — That was an awkward sea; and the funnel seems of my opinion, for it gives a complaining roar.

The wind blows stiffly from the nor'east, the sea runs high, we ship a deal of water, the night is dark and cold, and the shapeless passengers lie about in melancholy bundles, as if they were sorted out for the laundress; but for my own uncommercial part I cannot pretend that I am much inconvenienced by any of these things. A general howling, whistling, flopping, gurgling, and scooping, I am aware of, and a general knocking about of nature; but the impressions I receive are very vague. In a sweet, faint temper, something like the smell of damaged oranges, I think I should feel languidly benevolent if I had time. I have not time, because I am under a curious compulsion to occupy myself with the Irish melodies. "Rich and rare were the gems she wore," is the particular melody to which I find myself devoted. I sing it to myself in the most charming manner and with the greatest expression. Now and then I raise my head (I am sitting on the hardest of wet seats, in the most uncomfortable of wet attitudes, but I don't mind it), and notice that I am a whirling shut-tlecock between a fiery battledore of a light-house on the French coast and a fiery battledore of a light-house on the English coast; but I don't notice it particularly, except to feel envenomed in my hatred of Calais. Then I go on again: "Rich and rare were the ge-ems, she-e-e-e wore, And a bright gold ring on her wa-and she bo-ore, But oh, her beauty was fa-a-a-a-r beyond," — I am particularly proud of my execution here, when I become aware of another awkward shock from the sea, and another protest from the funnel, and a fellow-crea-ture at the paddle-box more audibly indisposed than I think he need be, — "Her sparkling gems, or snow-white wand, But oh, her beauty was fa-a-a-a-r beyond," — another awkward one here, and the fellow-creature with the umbrella down and picked up, — "Her spa-a-rkling ge-ems, or her Port! port! steady! steady! snow-white fellow-creature at the paddle-box very selfishly audible, bump, roar, wash, white wand."

Looking about me, I see the light of Cape Grinez well astern of the boat on the davits to leeward, and the light of Calais Harbour unde-niably at its old tricks, but still ahead and shining. Sentiments of for-giveness of Calais, not to say of attachment to Calais, begin to expand my bosom. I have weak notions that I will stay there a day or two on my way back. A faded and recumbent stranger, pausing in a profound revery over the rim of a basin, asks me what kind of place Calais is. I tell him (Heaven forgive me!) a very agreeable place indeed, — rather hilly than otherwise.

So strangely goes the time, and, on the whole, so quickly, — though still I seem to have been on board a week, — that I am bumped, rolled, gurgled, washed, and pitched into Calais Harbour before her maiden smile has finally lighted her through the Green Isle, When blest for ever is she who relied, On entering Calais at the top of the tide. For we have not to land tonight down among those slimy timbers, — covered with green hair, as if it were the mermaids' favourite combing-place, — where one crawls to the surface of the jetty, like a stranded shrimp; but we go steaming up the harbour to the Railway Station Quay. And as we go, the sea washes in and out among piles and planks, with dead heavy beats and in quite a furious manner (whereof we are proud); and the lamps shake in the wind, and the bells of Calais striking One seem to send their vibrations struggling against troubled air, as we have come struggling against troubled water. And now, in the sudden relief and wiping of faces, everybody on board seems to have had a prodigious double tooth out, and to be this very instant free of the dentist's hands. And now we all know for the first time how wet and cold we are, and how salt we are; and now I love Calais with my heart of hearts!

"Hôtel Dessin!" (but in this one case it is not a vocal cry; it is but a bright lustre in the eyes of the cheery representative of that best of inns.) "Hôtel Meurice!" "Hôtel de France!" "Hôtel de Calais!" "The Royal Hôtel, sir, Angaishe ouse!" "You going to Parry, sir?" "Your baggage, registair froo, sir?" Bless ye, my Touters, bless ye, my commissionnaires, bless ye, my hungry-eyed mysteries in caps of a military form, who are always here, day or night, fair weather or foul, seeking inscrutable jobs which I never see you get! Bless ye, my Custom-House officers in green and grey; permit me to grasp the welcome hands that descend into my travelling-bag, one on each side, and meet at the bottom to give my change of linen a peculiar shake up, as if it were a measure of chaff or grain! I have nothing to declare, Monsieur le Douanier, except that when I cease to breathe, Calais will be found written on my heart. No article liable to local duty have I with me, Monsieur l'Officier de l'Octroi, unless the overflowing of a breast devoted to your charming town should be in that wise chargeable. Ah! see at the gangway, by the twinkling lantern, my dearest brother and friend, he once of the Passport Office, he who collects the names! May he be for ever changeless in his buttoned black surtout, with his note-book in his hand, and his tall black hat surmounting his round, smiling, patient face! Let us embrace, my dearest brother. I am yours *à tout jamais* — for the whole of ever.

❧ *The first thing nearly everyone does when he arrives in France, especially for the first time, is head for Paris. The countryside, even the cities, between Paris and the coast or the airport are nothing but a backdrop for one's hopes and fears and, of course, one's fantasies of Paris. The well-traveled David Ogden Stewart was as fantastic, and nonsensical, a humorist as there's ever been. Here's how his typical American family, the Haddocks, experienced their train trip to Paris. And then a few words from the novelist Theodore Dreiser, who found tragedy in America and humor in France.*

Donald Ogden Stewart
In France at Last 1926

OH, but you can't know *Paris,*" murmured the nice lady sitting opposite Mr. Haddock in the first-class railroad compartment, "unless you live on the *rive gauche.*"

"That means *'the left bank,'*" immediately volunteered little Mildred — Mr. Haddock's daughter — who spoke French but with an accent.

"The left bank of *what?*" asked Mr. Haddock, wiping the perspiration from his forehead.

"Why — the *Seine,*" replied the lady, slightly condescendingly.

"A river in France," patiently explained the "little girl interpreter."

"Don't you suppose I know that?" demanded her father.

"No," replied Mildred promptly, and turning to the lady she announced, with a faint Continental shrug, *"Mon père* is in the lumber business and reads *très peu."*

"Mildred," said Mr. Haddock, reaching for a ball bat or a stout two-inch piece of iron pipe, "do you want papa to be cross?"

There had been, as a matter of fact, a considerable amount of condensed irritation in that railway carriage now speeding across France toward Paris. In the first place, Mrs. Haddock was feeling a little seasick now that the ocean voyage from America was over, and in the second place little Mildred didn't have any handkerchief, and in the third place Mr. Haddock had had an argument just before the train started with a French baggage porter which Mr. Haddock had lost, but which he was going to take to a Higher Court as soon as he could find out from Thomas Cook and Son or the American Express Company how to get to a Higher Court.

But anger and irritation were not what Mr. Haddock had come three thousand miles to find, and the country through which they were now passing was very sunny and very peaceful, and as he leaned back against the white crocheted head-rest and gazed out at the passing greenness of what looked a lot like wheat he gradually began to think of forgiving the French baggage porter for not speaking English.

"Well, Hattie," he said, patting his wife on the hand and pointing out of the window to a sign which read "Lucky Strike Cigarettes," "we're in France at last."

Just then the train shrieked its way into a long smoky tunnel.

"It looks a lot like America," was little Mildred's comment after the second minute of darkness, lighted only by a small blue lamp over their heads.

"I'm pretty sure it's France," said her father, "but we can always ask;" and when the compartment finally emerged once more into the sunshine he looked to the lady across from him for confirmation.

"Yes," she nodded, "it's France — *my* France." And she sighed deeply.

"It's *her* France, Hattie," said Mr. Haddock, a new note of respect in his voice.

Mrs. Haddock, surveying calmly the redness of many poppies amid the fresh verdure of French fields, was reminded (by the sight of a distant cemetery) to look up once more at the rack over Mr. Haddock's head to see if the bags were all there.

The bags *were* all there, but she was not sure she had locked *both* locks on the new suitcase after that silly examination at the Customs. It worried her, as did also the thought that it would have been safer to have packed her son's wife's picture in Mr. Haddock's pajamas. Broken glass was very dangerous, and if Mildred cut herself it would probably be impossible to get any Peroxide of Hydrogen, or Iodine in a place like Paris. Blood poisoning set in very rapidly, and before the doctor could arrive Mildred might lose the arm as far as the elbow. This would also undoubtedly bring on one of Mr. Haddock's heart attacks and she was not sure in which bag she had put Dr. Kendall's pills. She groaned, and removed a spot of egg or something from Mr. Haddock's left trouser leg.

But the faint distant pealing of a church bell in a square white stone tower carried her attention once more to the mellow French landscape, and her mind unconsciously began to run in tune to the eternal rhythm of the Old World.

"Will," she said, "I think you tipped that smoking room steward too much."

"A capital fellow," replied her husband, "with a wife and eight children in Baden-Baden — all girls."

"Fiddlesticks!" said Mrs. Haddock. "And you were a fool to give that French maid a cent. She didn't do a thing but make eyes at that silly bath steward all week."

"Ah," said Mr. Haddock, "the French — a wonderful little people," and he made as though to place an imaginary wreath at the tomb of the unknown soldier.

Theodore Dreiser
Building Up Paris 1911

A S the train sped on through the dark to Paris I fell to speculating on the wonders I was to see. Barfleur was explaining to me that in order to make my entrance into Paris properly gay and interesting, we were to dine at the Café de Paris and then visit the Folies-Bergère and afterwards have supper at the Abbaye Thélème.

I should say here that of all people I know Barfleur is as capable of creating an atmosphere as any — perhaps more so. The man lives so heartily in his moods, he sets the stage for his actions long beforehand, and then walks on like a good actor and plays his part thoroughly. All the way over — from the very first day we met in New York, I think — he was either consciously or unconsciously building up for me the glamour of smart and artistic life in Europe. Now these things are absolutely according to your capacity to understand and appreciate them; they are, if you please, a figment of the brain, a frame of mind. If you love art, if you love history, if the romance of sex and beauty enthralls you, Europe in places presents tremendous possibilities. To reach these ethereal paradises of charm, you must skip and blink and dispense with many things. All the long lines of commonplaces through which you journey must be as nothing. You buy and prepare and travel and polish and finally you reach the center of this thing which is so wonderful; and then, when you get there, it is a figment of your own mind. Paris and the Riviera are great realities — there are houses and crowds and people and great institutions and the remembrance and flavor of great deeds; but the thing that you get out of all this for yourself is born of the attitude or mood which you take with you. Toward gambling, show, romance, a delicious scene, Barfleur carries a special mood. Life is only significant because of these things. His great struggle is to avoid the dingy and the dull, and to escape if possible the penalties of encroaching age. I think he looks back on the glitter of his youth with a pathetic eye, and I know he looks forward into the dark with stoic solemnity. Just one hour of beauty, is his private cry, one more day of delight. Let the future take care of itself. He realizes, too, with the keenness of a realist, that if youth is not most vivid in yourself, it can sometimes be achieved through the moods of others. I know he found in me a zest and a curiosity and a wonder which he was keen to satisfy. Now he would see this thing over as he had seen it years before. He would observe me thrill and marvel, and so he would be able to thrill and marvel himself once more. He clung to me with delicious enthusiasm, and every now and then would say, "Come now, what are you thinking? I want to know. I am enjoying this as much as you are." He had a delicious vivacity which acted on me like wine.

As we neared Paris he had built this city up so thoroughly in my mood that I am satisfied that I could not have seen it with a realistic eye if I had tried. It was something — I cannot tell you what — Napoleon, the Louvre, the art quarter, Montmartre, the gay restaurants, the boulevards, Balzac, Hugo, the Seine and the soldiery, a score and a hundred things too numerous to mention and all greatly exaggerated. I hoped to see something which was perfect in its artistic appearance — exteriorly speaking. I expected, after reading George Moore and others, a wine-like atmosphere; a throbbing world of gay life; women of exceptional charm of face and dress; the bizarre, the unique, the emotional, the spirited. At Amiens I had seen enough women entering the trains to realize that the dreary commonplace of the English woman was gone. Instead the young married women that we saw were positively daring compared to what England could show — shapely, piquant, sensitive, their eyes showing a birdlike awareness of what this world has to offer. I fancied Paris would be like that, only more so; and as I look back on it now I can honestly say that I was not greatly disappointed. It was not all that I thought it would be, but it was enough. It is a gay, brilliant, beautiful city, with the spirit of New York and more than the distinction of London. It is like a brilliant, fragile child — not made for contests and brutal battles, but gay beyond reproach.

First Stop In France

*W*e stopped at the first café we came to, and entered. An old woman seated us at a table and waited for orders. The doctor said:

"Avez vous du vin?"

The dame looked perplexed. The doctor said again, with elaborate distinctness of articulation:

"Avez-vous du — vin!"

The dame looked more perplexed than before. I said:

"Doctor, there is a flaw in your pronunciation somewhere. Let me try her. Madame, avez-vous du vin? It isn't any use, doctor — take the witness."

"Madame, avez-vous du vin — ou fromage — pain — pickled pigs' feet — beurre — des oeufs — du boeuf — horse-radish, sourcrout, hog and hominy — *anything,* anything in the world that can stay a Christian stomach!"

She said:

"Bless you, why didn't you speak English before? — I don't know anything about your plagued French!" — *Mark Twain, 1869*

MAP OF PARIS

Paris

Mark Twain
Map of Paris 1871

THE accompanying map explains itself.

The idea of this map is not original with me, but is borrowed from the great metropolitan journals.

I claim no other merit for this production (if I may so call it) than that it is accurate. The main blemish of the city paper maps, of which it is an imitation, is that in them more attention seems paid to artistic picturesqueness than geographical reliability.

Inasmuch as this is the first time I ever tried to draft and engrave a map, or attempted anything in any line of art, the commendations the work has received and the admiration it has excited among the people have been very grateful to my feelings. And it is touching to reflect that by far the most enthusiastic of these praises have come from people who knew nothing at all about art.

By an unimportant oversight I have engraved the map so that it reads wrong end first, except to left-handed people. I forgot that in order to make it right in print, it should be drawn and engraved upside down. However, let the student who desires to contemplate the map stand on his head or hold it before a looking-glass. That will bring it right.

The reader will comprehend at a glance that that piece of river with the "High Bridge" over it got left out to one side by reason of a slip of the graving-tool, which rendered it necessary to change the entire course of the River Rhine, or else spoil the map. After having spent two days in digging and gouging at the map, I would have changed the course of the Atlantic Ocean before I would lose so much work.

I never had so much trouble with anything in my life as I had with this map. I had heaps of little fortifications scattered all around Paris at first, but every now and then my instruments would slip and fetch away whole miles of batteries, and leave the vicinity as clean as if the Prussians had been there.

The reader will find it well to frame this map for future reference, so that it may aid in extending popular intelligence, and in dispelling the widespread ignorance of the day.

OFFICIAL COMMENDATIONS.

It is the only map of the kind I ever saw.

U. S. GRANT.

―――

It places the situation in an entirely new light.

BISMARCK.

―――

I cannot look upon it without shedding tears.

BRIGHAM YOUNG.

―――

It is very nice large print.

NAPOLEON.

―――

My wife was for years afflicted with freckles, and, though everything was done for her relief that could be done, all was in vain. But, sir, since her first glance at your map, they have entirely left her. She has nothing but convulsions now.

J. SMITH.

To most people Paris is France and France is Paris, the eternal au courant. *Paris means so many things to so many: love, art, cuisine, rude men, insane drivers, and revolutionaries. The one thing everyone seems to agree on is that, unlike its namesake — the man who took Helen to Troy — Paris is a woman. Why it wasn't more aptly named after Helen herself is a mystery. At least they didn't call it Troy. Leave that to the classicists of upstate New York.*

Joseph Barry
Why Do You Love Me? 1951

EVER since there have been Americans, they have dreamed a dream and called it Paris. It began with Benjamin Franklin, who arrived in France in 1776 as the representative of the young republic, who later embraced Voltaire, who still later proposed marriage to the charming widow, Madame Helvetius — and was as charmingly refused. Ever since, American innocents abroad have been paying court in a clumsy mixture of French, English and chewing gum.

24

"Why do you love me?" she asks teasingly, and stays for the answer.

Why does Everyman and his American brother love Paris?

Like Oedipus before the Sphinx, we feel our life depends on the answer, although we know that love by definition is undefinable; by defining it, we finish it. So we talk about the first day we met. It's easier and it's truer. Or we turn to Thackeray who tells how one of his heroes fell in love one day in the Louvre:

She was standing, silent and majestic, in the center of one of the rooms of the statue gallery, and the very first glimpse of her struck one breathless with the sense of her beauty. I could not see the color of her eyes and hair exactly, but the latter is light, and the eyes, I should think, are gray. She may be some two and thirty years old, and she was born about two thousand years ago. Her name is Venus de Milo.

She is also called Paris. Paris, like Venus of Milo, was born — let us be courteously inexact — about 50 B.C. We love her with the passion of a young man and she returns our love with the ripeness of thirty-two and the wiles of two thousand.

Withal our Paris is not our fathers' Paris. But what is our love for her if it alters when it alteration finds? Worse than an ever-changing Paris would be a never-changing Paris. She would be as anomalous, as embarrassing to be with, as the Bonapartist one can see walking along the quais of the Seine, probing in the bookstalls, wearing the clothes and the sideburns of 1870, living on Rue Bonaparte, because for this man all time stopped with the end of the reign of Napoleon III. Paris wears yesterday's isms no longer than last season's clothes, the prewar ambiance gives way to the postwar as inevitably as surrealism to existentialism. Paris is a woman, not the tired old man called London. No hungry generations of lovers have trod her down. The body is as firm as Venus's, the spirit flares as brightly and the wit is sharper than ever.

Irvin S. Cobb
Indubitably a She-Town 1914

L ONDON is essentially a he-town, just as Paris is indubitably a she-town. That untranslatable, unmistakable something which is not to be defined in the plain terms of speech, yet which sets its mark on any long-settled community, has branded them both — the one as being masculine, the other as being feminine. For Paris the lily stands, the conventionalized, feminized lily; but London is a lion, a shag-headed, heavy-pawed British lion.

One thinks of Paris as a woman, rather pretty, somewhat regardless of morals and decidedly slovenly of person; craving admiration, but too indolent to earn it by keeping herself presentable; covering up the dirt on a piquant face with rice powder; wearing paste jewels in her earlobes in an effort to distract criticism from the fact that the ears themselves stand in need of soap and water.

A novelist is someone who, like Charles Dickens in the piece on Calais, can take a small idea or simple plot and draw it out like Silly Putty until it reaches 500 pages. A poet is someone who, like Hart Crane in the piece below, can take a city like Paris and squeeze it onto a postcard. And a critic is someone who, like the old Briton William Hazlitt, can't see the wonders of a city for its mud.

Hart Crane
And How! 1929

To Samuel Loveman (Postcard)

January 23, 1929

Dinners, soirées, poets, erratic millionaires, painters, translations, lobsters, absinthe, music, promenades, oysters, sherry, aspirin, pictures, Sapphic heiresses, editors, books, sailors. *And How!*

William Hazlitt
A Beast of a City 1826

PARIS is a beast of a city to be in — to those who cannot get out of it. Rousseau said well, that all the time he was in it, he was only trying how he should leave it. There is not a place in it where you can set your foot in peace or comfort, unless you can take refuge in one of their hotels, where you are locked up as in an old-fashioned citadel, without any of the dignity of romance. Stir out of it, and you are in danger of being run over every instant. Either you must be looking behind you the whole time, so as to be in perpetual fear of their hackney-coaches and cabriolets; or, if you summon resolution, and put off the evil to the last moment, they come up against you with a sudden acceleration of pace and a thundering noise, that dislocates your nervous system, till you are brought to yourself by having the same startling process repeated. Fancy yourself in London with the foot-path taken away, so that you are forced to walk along the middle of the streets with a dirty gutter running through them, fighting your way through coaches, waggons, and handcarts trundled along by large mastiff-dogs, with the houses twice as high, greasy holes for shop-windows, and piles of wood, green-stalls, and wheelbarrows placed at the doors, and the contents of wash-hand basins pouring out of a dozen stories — fancy all this and worse, and, with a change of scene, you are in Paris. The continual panic in which the passenger is kept, the alarm and the escape from it, the anger and the laughter at it, must have an effect on the Parisian character, and tend to make it the whiffling, skittish, snappish, volatile, inconsequential, unmeaning thing it is. The coachmen nearly drive over you in the streets, because they would not mind being driven over themselves — that is, they would have no fear of it the moment before, and would forget it the moment after. If an Englishman turns round, is angry, and complains, he is laughed at as a blockhead; and you must submit to be rode over in your national character. A horseman makes his horse curvet and capriole right before you, because he has no notion how an English lady, who is passing, can be nervous. They run up against you in the street out of mere heedlessness and hurry, and when you expect to have a quarrel (as would be the case in England) make you a low bow and slip on one side, to shew their politeness.

For many, Paris will always be the city that came out to welcome the American troops at the end of two World Wars. To them it means relief after great suffering, open, unarmed arms, women and song, jubilation, and a different sort of souvenir. The way you can always pick such people out of a crowd is to mention Paris offhandedly. Whoever breaks out in a tired rendition of "How ya gonna keep 'em down on the farm after they've seen Paree?" has been there before. Here are the memories of two World War I veterans, journalist Heywood Broun and humorist James Thurber.

Heywood Broun
The Franco-American Honeymoon 1919

THE day after the Americans marched in Paris one of the French newspapers referred to the doughboys as "Roman Caesars clad in khaki." The city set itself to liking the soldiers and everything American and succeeded admirably. Even the taxicab drivers refrained from overcharging Americans very much. School children studied the history of America and *The Star-Spangled Banner.* There were pictures of President Wilson and General Pershing in many shops and some had framed translations of the President's message to Congress. In fact, so eager were the French to take America to their hearts that they even made desperate efforts to acquire a working knowledge of baseball. *Excelsior,* an illustrated French daily, carried an action picture taken during a game played between American ambulance drivers just outside of Paris. The picture was entitled: "A player goes to catch the ball, which has been missed by the catcher," and underneath ran the following explanation: "We have given in our number of yesterday the rules of baseball, the American national game, of which a game, which is perhaps the first ever played in France, took place yesterday at Colombes between the soldiers of the American ambulances. Here is an aspect of the game. The pitcher, or thrower of balls, whom one sees in the distance, has sent the ball. The catcher, or *attrapeur,* who should restrike the ball with his wooden club, has missed it, and a player placed behind him has seized it in its flight."

The next day *L'Intransigeant* undertook the even more hazardous task of explaining American baseball slang. During the parade on the Fourth of July some Americans had greeted the doughboys with shouts of "ataboy." A French journalist heard and was puzzled. He returned to his office and looked in English dictionaries and various works of reference without enlightenment. Several English friends were unable to help him and an American who had lived in Paris for thirty years was equally at sea. But the reporter worked it out all by himself and the next day he wrote: "Parisians have been puzzled by the phrase 'ataboy' which Americans are prone to employ in moments of stress or emotion. The phrase is undoubtedly a contraction of 'at her boy' and may be closely approximated by *au travail, garçon.*" The writer followed with a brief history of the friendly relations of France and America and paid a glowing tribute to the memory of Lafayette . . .

The theaters gave the Americans almost as much recognition as the press. No musical show was complete without an American finale and each soubrette learned a little English, "I give you kees," or something like that, to please the doughboys. The vaudeville shows, such as those provided at the Olympia or the Alhambra, gave an even greater proportion of English speech. The Alhambra was filled with Tommies and doughboys on the night I went. Now and again the comedians had lapses of language and the Americans were forced to let jokes go zipping by without response. It was a pity, too, for they were good jokes even if French. Presently, however, a fat comedian fell off a ladder and laughter became general and international. . . .

And yet we Americans missed the old patter until there came a breath from across the sea. A low comedian came out and said to his partner in perfectly good English: "Well, didja like the show?" His partner said he didn't like the show. "Well, didja notice the trained seals?" persisted the low comedian and the lower comedian answered: "No, the wind was against 'em." Laughter long delayed overcame us then, but it was mingled with tears. We felt that we were home again. The French are a wonderful people and all that, of course, but they're so darn far away . . .

Restaurants as well as theaters were liberally sprinkled with men in the American uniform. The enlisted men ate for the most part in French barracks and seemed to fare well enough, although one doughboy, after being served with spinach as a separate course, complained: "I wish they'd get all the stuff on the table at once like we do in the army. I don't want to be surprised, I want to be fed." A young first lieutenant was scornful of French claims to master cookery. "Why, they don't know how to fry eggs," he said. "I've asked for fried eggs again and again and do you know what they do? They put 'em in a little dish and bake 'em.". . .

Practically every man on "permission" in Paris is making love to someone and usually in an open carriage or at the center table of a large restaurant. Nobody even turns around to look if a soldier walks along a street with his arm about a girl's waist. American officers, however, frowned on such exhibitions of demonstrativeness by doughboys and in one provincial town a colonel issued an order: "American soldiers will not place their arms around the waists of young ladies while walking in any of the principal thoroughfares of this town."

Still it was not possible to regulate romance entirely out of existence. "There was a girl used to pass my car every morning," said a sergeant chauffeur, "and she was so good looking that I got a man to teach me *bon jour,* and I used to smile at her and say that when she went by and she'd say *bon jour* and smile back. One morning I got an apple and I handed it to her and said *pour vous* like I'd been taught. She took it and came right back with, 'Oh, I'm ever so much obliged,' and there like a chump I'd been holding myself down to *bon jour* for two weeks."

There could be no question of the devotion of Paris to the American army. Indeed, so rampant was affection that it was occasionally embarrassing. One officer slipped in alighting from the elevator of his hotel and sprained his ankle rather badly. He was hobbling down one of the boulevards that afternoon with the aid of a cane when a large automobile dashed up to the curb and an elderly French lady who was the sole occupant beckoned to him and cried: *"Premier blessé."* The officer hesitated and a man who was passing stepped up and said: "May I interpret for you?" The officer said he would be much obliged. The volunteer interpreter talked to the old lady for a moment and then he turned and explained: "Madame is desirous of taking you in her car wherever you want to go, because she says she is anxious to do something for the first American soldier wounded on the soil of France."

The devotion of Paris was so obvious that it palled on one or two who grew fickle. I saw a doughboy sitting in front of the Café de la Paix one bright afternoon. He was drinking champagne of a sort and smoking a large cigar. The sun shone on one of the liveliest streets of a still gay Paris. It was a street made brave with bright uniforms. Brighter eyes of obvious noncombatants gazed at him with admiration. I was sitting at the next table and I leaned over and asked: "How do you like Paris?"

He let the smoke roll lazily out of his mouth and shook his head. "I wish I was back in El Paso," he said.

I found another soldier who was longing for Terre Haute. Him I came upon in the lounging room of a music hall called the Olympia. Two palpably pink ladies sat at the bar drinking cognac. From his table a few feet away the American soldier looked at them with high disfavor. Surprise, horror and indignation swept across his face in three waves as the one called Julie began to puff a cigarette after giving a light to Margot. He looked away at last when he could stand no more, and recognizing me as a fellow countryman, he began his protest.

"I don't like this Paris," he said. "I'm in the medical corps," he continued. "My home's in Terre Haute. In Indiana, you know. I worked in a drug store there before I joined the army. I had charge of the biggest soda fountain in town. We used to have as many as three men working there in summer sometimes. Right at a good business corner, you know. I suppose we had almost as many men customers as ladies."

"Why don't you like Paris?" I interrupted.

"Well, it's like this," he answered. "Nobody can say I'm narrow. I believe in people having a good time, but —" and he leaned nearer confidentially, "I don't like this Bohemia. I'd heard about it, of course, but I didn't know it was so bad. You see that girl there, the one in the blue dress smoking a cigarette, sitting right up to the bar. Well, you may believe it or not, but when I first sat down she came right over here and said, 'Hello, American. You nice boy. I nice girl. You buy me a drink.' I never saw her before in my life, you understand, and I didn't even look at her till she spoke to me. I told her to go away or I'd call a policeman and have her arrested. I've been in Paris a week now, but I don't think I'll ever get used to this Bohemia business. It's too effusive, that's what I call it. I'd just like to see them try to get away with some of that business in Terre Haute."

The high tide in the American conquest of Paris came one afternoon in July. I got out of a taxicab in front of the American headquarters in the Rue Constantine and found that a big crowd had gathered in the Esplanade des Invalides. Now and again the crowd would give ground to make room for an American soldier running at top speed. One of them stood almost at the entrance of the courtyard of "Invalides." His back was turned toward the tomb for Napoleon and he was knocking out flies in the direction of the Seine. Unfortunately it was a bit far to the river and no baseball has yet been knocked into that stream. It was a new experience for Napoleon though. He has heard rifles and machine guns and other loud reports in the streets of Paris, but for the first time there came to his ears the loud sharp crack of a bat swung against a baseball. Since he could not see from out the tomb the noise may have worried the emperor. Perhaps he thought it was the British winning new battles on other cricket fields. But again he might not worry about that now. He might hop up on one toe as a French caricaturist pictured him and cry: *"Vive l'Angleterre!"*

One of the men in the crowd which watched the batting practice was a French soldier headed back for the front. At any rate he had his steel helmet on and his equipment was on his back. His stripes showed that he had been in the war three years and he had the Croix de Guerre with two palms and the Médaille Militaire. His interest in the game grew so high at last that he put down his pack and his helmet and joined the outfielders. The second or third ball hit came in his direction. He ran about in a short circle under the descending ball and at the last moment he thrust both hands in front of his face. The ball came between them and hit him in the nose, knocking him down.

His nose was a little bloody, but he was up in an instant grinning. He left the field to pick up his trench hat and his equipment. The Americans shouted to him to come back. He understood the drift of their invitation, but he shook his head. *"C'est dangereux,"* he said, and started for the station to catch his train for the front.

James Thurber
Souvenirs 1957

BACK in Paris, I made a brief survey of the souvenirs collected by Americans I knew. One man had brought from somewhere a machine gun, which he kept in his hotel room and left there when he went home. Legend had it that the upraised sword of the equestrian statue of George Washington in the Place d'Iéna had been replaced nine times, and one overenthusiastic vandal had been arrested while attempting to take one of the gilt cherubs from the superstructure of the bridge of Alexandre III across the Seine. A sailor I know collected, with the aid of chisel and screwdriver, ornate locks from old doors and gates, and his trophies must have weighed a good hundred pounds. A doughboy who fancied bronze and marble busts in museums was less successful. It was rumored, in the days of the Great Hunt, that not more than five servicemen were admitted to Napoleon's tomb at one time. Everybody heard, and retold, the wonderful myth of the bold and enterprising soldier in the Louvre who had got away with the arms of the Venus de Milo and the head of the Winged Victory.

ﻬParis will always be Paris, but even Paris is not the same all year long. It has five seasons, each with a hefty share of différence. There is Springtime: April in Paris, blossoms, everyone out in the streets, dancing and music. There is Summer: warm and pleasant, buzzing with activity. There is Autumn: wet, chilly, but free of tourists at last. There is Winter: barren, frigid . . . Wait, how can anyone talk that way about a woman. Even in winter, Paris is hot-blooded; one must simply work harder to find the warmth. Finally, there is the season *that only Paris seems to have: August, when the proud, passionate woman becomes a desert even the Foreign Legion deserts (not to mention Art Buchwald).*

Art Buchwald
Survival in August 1960

A s everyone knows, August is the month when every Frenchman in Paris goes on vacation. On July 31, all the storekeepers slam down their iron shutters; electricians, plumbers, and garage men pack in their tools; and factories, offices, stores, government buildings, restaurants, and dry-cleaning establishments shut down for the entire month.

In previous years, when the Parisians returned in September, they found the skeletons of many foreigners in positions indicating they had been trying to get into a closed bakery, a drugstore, or a laundry.

Among the more tragic cases was one of a man who was found in front of a restaurant, clutching his half-eaten Diners' Club credit card in one hand. The body was still warm and indicated the man had expired only twenty-four hours before the restaurant reopened for the autumn season.

Another was of a woman who was found floating underneath the ceiling of her apartment. Next to her was a piece of paper with the number of a plumber on it. Apparently the woman had been trying all month to get the plumber, and finally the water got too high for her to reach the phone. The police said phoning wouldn't have done her any good as the plumber was in Brittany.

Still another case was that of a tourist whose car broke down at the Place de la Concorde. Instead of leaving the car to seek out help, he remained behind the wheel, waiting for someone from the Automobile Club to tow him away. Naturally, no one came; and finally, without water, he perished, not realizing he was only a few yards from the Seine.

Another tourist became so desperate because all the laundries were closed that he broke into a locked Bendix laundromat and tried to wash his own shirt. He was caught and is now doing twenty years at the Santé Prison.

And who will ever forget the day in August 1955 when four people were killed and thirty-six injured on the Champs Elysées fighting over a lone taxicab which had come in from Deauville by mistake?

Every year the situation has become grimmer, but this year a group of foreigners who have to remain in Paris to take care of visiting firemen have decided to do something about it.

The first idea was to appeal to the International Red Cross in Geneva, but the appeal met with no success, because the International Red Cross turned it over to the French Red Cross, and everyone at the French Red Cross was going on vacation.

So the group of foreigners decided to form a nonprofit organization called the Society of People Stuck in Paris in August or, as it will soon be known, SOPSIPIA.

SOPSIPIA, in its first meeting decided to issue survival kits at cost. The survival kits for men include a Dacron shirt, a Wash 'n' Dri suit, a role of film, a bottle of Brut champagne, a croissant, three haricots verts, a copy of *Lady Chatterley's Lover,* and a Do-It-Yourself Strip Tease Act.

The women's survival kit includes a box of Kleenex, a box of Tide, a set of post cards, a brioche, a home permanent, a green salad, another box of Kleenex, and a glass string bag for window shopping.

At its first meeting, the committee also decided to set up free Vichyssoise kitchens in front of Thomas Cook and the American Express.

Courses in survival will be given at Maxim's and the Tour d'Argent, and a place on the banks of the Seine will be set aside for wives who wish to do laundry.

Many American companies are co-operating with SOPSIPIA. Pan American Airways is running a contest in Paris, in which the winner of the first prize will receive an American plumber for a week-end.

TWA is also running a contest. The winner of its contest will have his suit flown to New York for dry cleaning.

These and many more things make for one of the most exciting Augusts Paris has seen in years. I only wish I could be here to see it. But unfortunately I'm going on vacation.

A Child's Perspective

I was extremely taken up with the soft
red cushions of the arm-chairs, which
it took one half an hour to subside into after
sitting down, — with the exquisitely polished
floor of the salon, and the good-natured
French 'Boots' (more properly 'Brushes'), who
skated over it in the morning till it became as
reflective as a mahogany table, — with the
pretty court full of flowers and shrubs in beds
and tubs, between our rez-de-chaussée
windows and the outer gate, — with a nice
black servant belonging to another family,
who used to catch the house-cat for me; and
with an equally good-natured *fille de
chambre,* who used to catch it back again, for
fear I should teaze it (her experience of
English boy-children having made her
dubious of my intentions); — all these things
and people I remember, — and the Tuileries
garden, and the 'Tivoli' gardens, where my
father took me up and down a 'Russian
mountain', and I saw fireworks of the finest.
But I remember nothing of the Seine, nor of
Notre Dame, nor of anything in or even out
of the town except the windmill on Mont
Martre. — *John Ruskin, 1889*

❧Sightseeing

❧*There's so much to see in Paris, where do you start? The Eiffel Tower, Notre Dame, Montmartre, the Louvre, the Pompidou Center, the Invalides, the Left Bank, the Seine, the nightlife, even Dickens' favorite place, the Morgue (it was also the choice of 19th-century American humorist Bill Nye: "I go to the Morgue whenever I feel depressed," he wrote. "There is peace. Even the Frenchmen are quiet."). Some of you will only be passing through Paris on the way to the provinces or other capitals. With the daredevil nature of the Parisian cabbie, you will try to do Paris in a day. It is for you, the nibbler and the sportsman-tourist, that Ring Lardner and Art Buchwald, respectively (but not respectfully), wrote the following pieces.*

Ring Lardner
Me and the Madam in Paris 1925

WE left Deauville one morning at eight o'clock and reached gay Paris at eleven o'clock. I had both wired and written for reservations, but the head clerk hadn't never heard of me. Finally, however, he says to register and he would do what he could in a couple of hours.

Well, anyway, while we was waiting, I took the madam over to the Seine which is a big river running right through the town, and also showed her the Eiffel Tower which she said what is it for and I couldn't answer, and I also showed her the Louvre and the Tuileries and finally took her to Maxim's for lunch and it was the first time she ever seen ladies standing up to the bar amongst the boys and several of the ladies smiled at me and she wanted to know where had I met them, so I says they probably recognized me from my pictures.

We got our room after lunch and the man that showed us up to it said that Gloria Swanson and Jackie Coogan was stopping at our hotel though not together, but anyway we stayed in our room all afternoon expecting maybe one of them would call up. The phone didn't ring however, and finally we went down to dinner and then to the Folies-Bergère, which the gals comes out in one scene all dressed up like Eve. In the final scene they have a pool on the stage and the Tiller Girls walk down steps into it clear over their heads. The wife made the remark that it wouldn't hurt none of the costumes in the show if they was submerged a while.

Well, to make a short story out of a long story, why, during this stay in gay Paris we took in all the Montmartre night joints like the Dead Bat and so forth and the only shock I got was when they brought the check around. All the music was American jazz and all the conversation was American and English, though one of the newspaper men told me that they's some old time Parisians that still speaks French.

Art Buchwald
The Six-Minute Louvre 1957

ANY sportsman will tell you that the only three things to see in the Louvre are the "Winged Victory of Samothrace," the "Venus de Milo" and the "Mona Lisa." The rest of the sculpture and paintings are just so much window dressing for the Big Three, and one hates to waste time in the Louvre when there is so much else to see in Paris.

Ever since the Louvre acquired these works of art, amateurs from all over the world have been trying to cut down the time it takes to see them. Before the war the world record was held by three Scandinavians, who had managed to make the course in seven minutes thirty-three seconds. This record stood until 1935, when a Britisher, Mergenthaller Waisleywillow, paced by his Welsh wife, did it in seven minutes flat. Waisleywillow in his first attempt made it in six minutes and forty-nine seconds, but was disqualified when he forgot to make a complete circle of the "Venus de Milo."

The record stood until 1938, when a Stockholm man, known as the Swedish Cannonball, introduced sneakers and made it in six minutes and twenty-five seconds.

That record stood during the war years, and it wasn't until 1947 that an attempt was made to beat the Cannonball. This time, because of the travel restrictions in Europe, the Americans had the course to themselves. The first one to take the Blue Riband to America was Tex Houston, from Oklahoma, who shaved two seconds off the record. In

1949 a track star from Miami University (Ohio) made it in six minutes and fourteen seconds. In 1951, the Australians took the title away from the Americans with a six-minute-twelve-second Louvre.

By this time everyone was talking about a six-minute Louvre. Scientists said that under perfect conditions, with a smooth floor, excellent lighting and no wind, it could be done. But for four years no one was able to beat the Australians.

Then one Sunday I was tipped off that an American tourist was going to try for the record. His name was Peter Stone and he had made several previous attempts that had failed. Mr. Stone has been cited in many magazines and newspapers for a famous remark. After studying the "Winged Victory" for an hour, he said, "It will never fly."

He also was once asked to leave the Louvre when he said in a loud voice in front of a group of tourists who were looking at the "Mona Lisa": "I know the fellow who has the original."

Stone had brought his trainer along with him. He was wearing special indoor track shoes, and he had emptied his pockets of anything that would weigh him down. In choosing Sunday morning for the test he had banked on several things. One was that no tickets are required to get in and he would not lose precious seconds at the ticket booth.

Another was that the Louvre is pretty empty on Sunday mornings and most of the halls would be clear. In order to comply with all the rules, Stone had to get out of a taxi and tell the driver to wait. Then he had to rush into the museum, make the course, and get back in the taxi. The taxi had to be four feet away from the curb before he was officially clocked. Timekeepers from the American Express, Thomas Cook & Son and the French Bureau de Tourisme were on hand.

Stone received last-minute instructions from his trainer.

"Whatever you do, keep away from the 'Rape of the Sabines' or you're a goner."

Stone wiped his track shoes in the box of resin that the Louvre keeps at the door for tourists and then got into the taxi. A gun went off and he jumped out of the taxi and rushed into the museum. The rule of the course is you must walk; you cannot run. Keeping his eyes straight ahead, he whizzed past the Salle Denon. At the foot of the Daru staircase, with just a glance at "Winged Victory," he turned left and rushed down two small flights of stairs past the rotunda straight to the "Venus de Milo." He circled the statue completely and headed back toward the "Winged Victory," shortcutting through the Roman and Greek antiquity rooms. His time was a fantastic one minute and fifty-eight seconds to the "Venus."

Stone took the stairs two at a time, stopped for two seconds in front of the "Winged Victory." He had a choice of two routes: the Salle Daru, where Napoleon I was being crowned, or the Salle Sept Mètres, where the Italian school was hung. He chose the Salle Daru, paused only for a second at the Napoleon painting and then rushed into the Grande Galerie, where "Mona Lisa" was waiting. In thirty seconds he was at the painting. The rules state that a contestant must make some innocuous tourist remark at the painting.

Stone said, "I don't see what's so great about it," and then wheeled, this time taking the Salle Sept Mètres. He rushed down the stairs, not even bothering this time to look at the "Winged Victory," hightailed it through the Salle Denon and was out in the street and in a taxi before you could say Leonardo da Vinci. As the taxi pulled away a gun was set off and Stone's time was recorded at five minutes fifty-six seconds, a new world tourist record. The Blue Riband was brought back to America.

Turning down offers from magazines and travel agencies which wanted to use him for testimonial advertisements, Stone modestly gave much of the credit to his trainer.

"The next record I'm going after is St. Peter's in Rome," he said in an exclusive interview. "And then, who knows — perhaps I'll try the Tower of London. They say you can't do it in less than four minutes. Well, let's just see."

The champ threw his arms around his mother and the photographers started taking pictures.

✎ *Few guidebooks offer the peculiar, some might say perverse, point of view; they all talk to the average Joe and Jane's interests or, at least, to the interests the average Joe and Jane discuss in public. For example, in the section on Notre Dame they point out its architectural aspects, tell stories from the great moments of its history, and, perhaps, mention Victor Hugo's hunchback, assuring Americans that he was not one of the Fighting Irish. When humorist Donald Ogden Stewart visited, the results were different: "when we stopped in front of the great cathedral I quietly and impressively announced to her, 'that church is Notre Dame, mother.' She wasn't gazing in the right direction, so I repeated, 'Look, mother — Notre Dame!' And then, instead of paying any attention to the cathedral, she pointed gleefully to a* nearby tree and said, 'There's an English sparrow — just like the ones in Columbus!'"

Here are a few tours and guides the guidebooks could never imagine, from Jules Janin's involuntary tour of Parisian architecture to Christopher Morley's visit to a famous graveyard, from Don Marquis' Old Soak and archy the cockroach to Homer Croy's Oklahoman, who brings his all-American attitudes to bear on everything he sees.

Homer Croy
The Champs-Elysées 1926

A T first the family wandered awkwardly and ill at ease among the mirrors, gold chairs, and ostentation of the hotel. They saw men with strange clothes and uniforms, men with medals spread across their breasts, men with decorations, men with beards and alien manners; women bright with jewelry and women in black moving slowly and majestically along the softly carpeted halls; young girls, rouged and powdered, leading dogs, flashed in and out, so much at home, so calm and sure of themselves. The family heard a babble of tongues they couldn't understand, and now and then they heard a language which seemed vaguely familiar; after a time they would recognize it. It was the English aristocracy talking.

"The first thing we must see," said Mrs. Peters the next day, "is the Champs-Elysées, because that is what the people back home are going to ask about. It is the most famous and beautiful avenue in the world."

Getting into a taxi, they started up the busy, teeming street. The sun was shining and Paris was at its best. They turned into the Place de la Concorde and around them rose the magnificent stretch of buildings in all their gray glory; in the center of the Place, the Obelisk, commemorating the glory of Cleopatra in Egypt, stood brooding as if laughing at this gay, hurrying, absurd world. "Once Cairo and Alexandria were just as foolish," it seemed to say. "Go on — you won't last long." To the left across the river was the somber, massive, secretive Chamber of Deputies, and faintly outlined at the far end of the avenue was the Arch of Triumph smiling back at the Obelisk as if to say: "Don't take it too seriously. The human race is often foolish and absurd, but it's on its way up." And between, a whirling welter of cars dashed by in all directions, sometimes stopping, pausing a moment, then darting away again in some mad, fantastic race, like water bugs on a pond.

Don Marquis
Gargle Oils 1925

PARIS, Sept. 18. — Well, theyer is lots of arkytexture in Paris, almost every other bldg. you see is all arkytextured up in one way or the other, I never seen so many churches in all my born days, not even in Brooklin, theyer uset to be as many breweries as theyer was churches in Brooklin but now the noes have it.

Neerly all these Paris churches is erected to the memry of Saint Somebody, or other, and for the sake of argyment this Saint was as a usual thing massicured way back in the erly days.

Theyer was Saint Denny, he must of been an Irrishman by his name, they cut his head off and he picked it up and beat it away from thare and carried his head in his hands for miles and miles, Pierre the showfure told me about it, and finally he stubbed his toe on them cobblestones and fell down, but his head kept on a rolling and a rolling and whare it stopped they errected a church to his memry.

Well, Al says, he couldn't of been an Irrishman, if he had of been an Irrishman he would have swung on somebody with that head and beaned them, you never seen an Irrishman that wouldn't of swung on somebody.

Then thare was Saint Notary Dom, his church has been all arkytextured up with gargle oils, they are sticking out over the roof of it, with theyer necks stretched and theyer mouths open, they are mean looking goofs.

Well, Al says, why do they call them gargle oils.

Doant be an iggnoramus, I told him, annybody ought to see they call them gargle oils because they are cleering theyer throats. They are carved that natural you can almost hear them hawk and spit.

I will tell the world them gargle oils are nothing to look at after a feller has had from cat to seece weeskies, you can't quit looking at them and you go and get seece more shots and look at them again and then they begin to get pursonal the way they wiggle theyer heads and wink at you.

Poor Al he gets a little bit lit up the other evening and he goes up on top of a place called Mongmart and he gets down on his hands and knees at the edge of the bluff and stretches his neck out over the city and begins to whine and bark and make noises like a trayned blood hound in a uncle Tom's cabin show.

What in the name of a hell are you doing that for Al, I asks him, you better snap out of it.

You leeve me be, Clem, he says, I am a gargle oil. I guess I got a right to be a gargle oil if I want to.

You ain't as young as you uset to be, you will have lumbague in the small of your back tomorrow morning, I tells him.

Lumbague or no lumbague, he says, I can lick any other gargle oil my size in Paris.

The only way I could get him started for home was to coax him onto the top of Pierre's taxi cab, he wouldn't get inside of it, and he stretched his self over the edge and played he was a gargle oil and I had to set on his legs to keep him from rolling off, and that way we went through all the prinssiple streets.

And Pierre would stop his cab every time we come to one of them side walk cafes, and Al would ask if any gent would like to feed the gargle oils, and purty soon some fellers we never seen afore got cabs and come along with us and played they was gargle oils too and that gargle oil parade crossed over the river and we picked up some stewdents over on the bool mish and they played they was gargle oils and it got to be quite a sport by midnight, with Al leeding the percession and evry time we come to another cafe he would say, I'm a gargle oil, I'm a gargle oil, come and throw hoops at the gargle oils, the gargle oil you ring is the gargle oil you get.

The way some Americans drink in Paris is enough to make you a frend of moderashin for life, it was 4 oclock a m in the morning afore I got that Al to bed and I says I am ashamed of you. He says you leeve me be, my shoulders is itching like wings is starting. If it wasn't for his fool friends holding him down, he says, he would fly over the city.

Jules Janin
The Englishman's Visit
to Paris 1843

A YOUNGER brother of Lord S ——, the honest and learned vicar of a village near London, had taken leave of his people, to pay a visit to Paris, *the city of wonders,* as it was called there. This Englishman, though very learned, was a man of exquisite taste, but somewhat absent in mind. For a long time, he had had a great wish to see, and to perambulate, and to study the great capital. At last he arrived in Paris, on one of those clear summer nights, which have almost the transparency of day. After having walked our streets, for some time, followed by a man carrying his baggage, he ordered his guide to take him to a good hotel. Led by him to a comfortable house, our Englishman passed the night; but what strange dreams appeared before his eyes! He did not rouse himself, till ten o'clock in the morning, so badly had he slept. He then dressed himself in haste, fearing lest Paris had taken flight, and went out without knowing the name of the street, or of the hotel where he had passed the night. His emotion was so great, his curiosity so strongly excited, that he walked for a long time, to the right, to the left, before him, through a thousand streets great and small, through a thousand passages and a thousand turnings; he went and came, he returned, he passed bridges, he stopped, he admired, he was astonished; in a word, he wandered so far and so long, that at the end of three good hours' walking, he was far from his hotel, lost, thoroughly lost, without any means of recovering himself. What should he do?

Happily, this worthy William S—— was a man of much composure, which did not forsake him, even on this, his first day of enthusiasm and wandering. As soon as he perceived that he had really lost himself in this great city, he began to reflect on the best means of discovering this street, of the name of which he was in perfect ignorance, and this hotel which he might be said to have scarcely seen, except at night. Remember, that in this hotel he had his clothes. What do I say? his clothes! he had left his name and passport. — His name and passport? he had left his personal liberty. — His personal liberty? he had left better than that, he had left his purse. It was a grave and pressing emergency.

To tell the truth, the first moment of confusion and embarrassment was most painful. But our hero was not discouraged. He waited where he was, till chance should bring him some worthy, honest Frenchman, honest enough to encourage him, acute enough to give him good counsel. Just then, chance, which is not always an enemy, sent that way a kind, clever young man, who had studied architecture at Rome, and who after having built upon paper at the school, I know not how many temples, studies, theatres, amphitheatres, baths, aqueducts, porticos, lyceums, parthenons, pantheons, &c. &c., thought himself only too happy, to have chimneys to repair, and houses to replaster in the Rue Mouffetard.

The stranger accosted the young artist, with the smile of an honest man, which is perhaps the best recommendation one can have, in any city, or in any latitude.

Sir, said the Englishman, will you be kind enough to listen to me with indulgence, and not laugh too much at my simplicity. Sir, I am an honest English clergyman, and had never quitted my village, until, urged by an unfortunate curiosity, I crossed the strait expressly and solely to see Paris. I arrived yesterday evening, and was taken to a hotel where I passed the night. This morning, in my enthusiasm, and my desire to see every thing, I left my hotel, without remembering that I must return there this evening; so that I am lost, hungry, and. . .

Sir, said the architect to the Englishman, the case is an awkward one. Let us begin by breakfast.

And they entered a café.

While breakfasting, the young man said to the Englishman —

Well Sir! have you not at least some indications by the help of which we can discover between us, this street and this hotel?

Sir, said the Englishman, with a strange look of assurance, that is just what I was about to tell you, when you offered me breakfast so àpropos. I am not as utterly lost as you may perhaps think me; for now, I remember perfectly, that the house where I passed the night is near a kind of Grecian temple, which I saw shining in the moon's light; you know, Sir, large white columns mingled with flights of steps, the whole being surmounted by long stove funnels, which, to tell you the truth, appeared to me but little Athenian.

At these words, the young artist, who thoroughly understood all the mysteries and all the secrets of our architecture, burst into a long fit of laughing.

What! said he to the amazed Englishman, have you no other indications than that? Do you not know whether there was a butcher or a perfumer in your street? You are no nearer your mark, Sir!

Sir, said the Englishman, looking somewhat piqued, does it so happen in your country, that there are fewer butchers' shops than Grecian temples?

Exactly so, Sir. In Paris, we know the number of our butchers' stalls; there are only three hundred; but we do not know the number of our Grecian temples. But stop, said he, you and I will soon try the truth of this; and we have not much time left, for visiting all our Grecian temples.

And they immediately set about seeking for this hotel, situated at the corner of a Grecian temple.

They were then not far from the Théâtre Italien, which is certainly a Grecian temple, with white columns surmounted by magnificent stove funnels.

Is that your temple? said he to the Englishman.

That's my temple! answered he, joyfully. But alas! if he had recognized his temple, he could not find his hotel.

I told you so! cried the triumphant artist.

When they had made the entire tour of the Théâtre Italien, and of these columns, the spaces between which are filled with joinery and windows, so useful are columns under our beautiful Grecian sky;

Do not be discouraged, Sir, said the young man, there is close by, another Grecian temple.

And turning to the right, they went to the Madeleine.

Here is my Grecian temple! said the Englishman, with some uneasiness.

I am afraid this is not your Grecian temple, replied the artist; it is a catholic church, sir.

You are right, said the Englishman, when he had looked on both sides for his hotel; this is not my Grecian temple.

Shall we take a cabriolet? replied his companion, for we have so many Grecian temples to visit!

They mounted a cabriolet. By this time, the Englishman felt rather confused.

The architect, for an instant undecided to what Grecian temple to take the stranger, began to remember, that there was a hotel of Windsor or of London, of the Prince Regent, or some other national hotel not far from the Chamber of Deputies, and so he led William to the Chamber.

Sir, said he, this is a magnificent Grecian temple! look at the columns! look at the flights of steps! look at the stove funnels!

You are right, said the Englishman. And stop, here is my hotel.

But at this Hotel de Windsor, they did not recognise the Englishman.

We must look for another Grecian temple, said Ernest. (Our artist's name was Ernest.)

Ernest, who in his capacity of a man of merit and talent, had a chimney to rebuild in the rue de l'Odéon, took his companion to the Odéon.

Here, said he to the unfortunate William, is another magnificent Grecian temple, ornamented with magnificent chimnies. It is a tragedy theatre, Sir, and there is no lack of hotels in this neighbourhood.

But the Englishman recognised, neither his hotel nor his Grecian temple . . .

But if the Englishman was unhappy, Ernest on his part began to be impatient. Where should he find this Grecian temple, and this colonnade descended in a direct line from the Portico or the Parthenon?

Shall we dine in the palais royal? said the young man to William.

They went to dine in the palais royal.

Here are columns! said Ernest to the Englishman.

Whilst dining, they heard people talking of M. Berryer, who is the column of the bar; M. de Lamartine, the column of the library; Mlle. Fanny Ellsler and Mlle. Taglioni, the two Ionic columns of the opera; Mlle. Mars, the column of the Théâtre Français; Meyerbeer and Rossini, the two columns of music; and a crowd of other columns, parliamentary, eloquent, nervous, and governmental, enough to make a Grecian temple that would reach from Paris to St. Petersburgh.

Here are *columns* enough, said Ernest.

When they had dined, they went for coffee, to the *Café des Mille-Colonnes*. The Englishman could bear it no longer.

Sir, said Ernest to him, shall we go to the Opera? That is a Grecian temple, at least; it has several staircases, many columns, and above all, many chimneys. Let us go there.

But at the Opera I shall not find my hotel, said the Englishman.

At the Opera, replied Ernest, you will find many Grecian temples.

In going to the Opera, they crossed the Rue Richelieu.

Here is a temple half Grecian, said Ernest, as he pointed out the square columns of the Théâtre Français.

They passed before an overthrown building, pulled down only the day before.

Stop, Sir, said Ernest, there was formerly on this spot a magnificent Grecian temple; it was an expiatory monument for the duke de Berri, so unworthily assassinated, and whom the revolution of July has deprived of his monument, just as it has suppressed the celebration of the twelfth of January, in memory of Louis XVI., the martyr king.

However, it was late, the moon had risen. In passing the corner of the Rue Richelieu;

I have it! cried Ernest, transported with joy.

And he led him to the Place de la Bourse, just opposite the Théâtre Vaudeville.

There is a Grecian temple! said Ernest.

My Grecian temple was much larger, replied the Englishman.

In that case, turn round, said Ernest.

The Englishman wheeled about. Oh joy! he was before that Grecian temple called the Bourse.

This time, *it is* my Grecian temple, said the Englishman. And he at once entered his hotel.

When he returned to his village, William was asked;

What do you think of Paris?
Paris, said he, is an assemblage of shops and Grecian temples.

Don Marquis
archy at the tomb of napoleon 1927

     paris france
     i went over to
     the hotel des invalides
     today and gazed on
     the sarcophagus of the
     great napoleon
     and the thought came
     to me as i looked
     down indeed it
     is true napoleon
     that the best goods
     come in the smallest
     packages here are
     you napoleon with
     your glorious course
     run and here is
     archy just in the
     prime of his career
     with his greatest
     triumphs still before
     him neither one of us
     had a happy youth
     neither one of us
     was welcomed socially at
     the beginning of his
     career neither one of
     us was considered much
     to look at
     and in ten thousand years from
     now perhaps what you said and did
     napoleon will be
     confused with what
     archy said and did
     and perhaps the burial
     place of neither will be

known napoleon looking
down upon you
I wish to ask you now
frankly as one famous
person to another
has it been worth
all the energy
that we expended all the
toil and trouble and
turmoil that it cost us
if you had your life
to live over
again bonaparte would
you pursue the star
of ambition
i tell you frankly
bonaparte that i myself
would choose the
humbler part
i would put the temptation
of greatness aside
and remain an ordinary
cockroach simple
and obscure but alas
there is a destiny that
pushes one forward
no matter how hard
one may try to resist it
i do not need to
tell you about that
bonaparte you know as
much about it as i do
yes looking at it in
the broader way neither
one of us has been to blame
for what he has done
neither for his great
successes nor his great mistakes
both of us napoleon
were impelled by some
mighty force external to
ourselves we are both to

be judged as great forces of
nature as tools in the
hand of fate rather than as
individuals who willed to
do what we have done
we must be forgiven
napoleon
you and i
when we have been
different from the common
run of creatures
i forgive you as i know
that you would forgive
me could you speak to me
and if you and i
napoleon forgive and
understand each other
what matters it if all
the world else find
things in both of us that
they find it hard
to forgive and understand
we have been
what we have been
napoleon and let them laugh that off
well after an hour or so of
meditation there i left
actually feeling that i
had been in communion
with that great spirit and
that for once in my
life i had understood and been
understood
and i went away feeling
solemn but likewise
uplifted mehitabel the
cat is missing
                    archy

Christopher Morley
A Paris Crowd 1926

ONE of the delights [of travel] is that you know no one and no one knows you. That free and solitary passage among multitudes can never quite be attained at home; perhaps only in a foreign city where different language and different aspect of things turn the mind in upon itself for its needed reassurance and composure. There is something divine in the sensation of your secret swim through this human ocean. You carry your own heavy and fragile burden of hopes, anxieties, joys, remorses, and you know that you will not, from *café crême* at breakfast to *café cognac* at midnight, encounter any one who has the faintest concern to share or jostle that curious load. So must the gods have walked among men. And you marvel at those voyagers who hasten to inscribe themselves in the register at the American Express office, to have their names and hotels chronicled by the *Herald*—in short, who so readily abandon that most rare and refined of human pleasures, the perfect incognito.

Perhaps the most thrilling crowd in Paris is the crowd in *Père Lachaise* — the crowd of the dead. I wanted specially to see again the monument Aux Morts in its little green ravine. There were some particular graves I should have liked to see, too; but I felt it would be the depth of bad manners to go hunting them out with the aid of a plan. In that perfect democracy of silence only the vulgarest of snobs would be picking and choosing, looking for "famous" tombs. It was a grey drizzling day, the stone-ranked hill was very solitary, and I strolled at random, content (so I found myself rather gruesomely putting it) with the monuments I happened to pass. I will be honest: I had a faint velleity to see the grave of Oscar O'Flaherty Fingalls Wills Wilde (I believe he is buried there) because any man devoted to publishing has a natural interest in the writer who has caused more bogus *de luxe* sets than any other (except perhaps Maupassant?). I wanted to see if the Epstein sphinx which once caused such a row was finally erected. But I didn't find it; and was more than compensated by discovering the tall shaft that the City of Paris has put in memory of her municipal workmen — pipe layers, car conductors, electricians, and others — who have lost their lives in the course of duty.

I don't know (perhaps Sir Thomas Browne or Lord Bacon were the only prowlers who have known) exactly what one feels among these crumblings of mortality. What is our æsthetic of the dust? Is it a small and shamed superiority, to be still topside the gravel? or is it even more disgusting self-pity? At any rate, that noble Aux Morts, unspeakably beautiful tableau of human grief and courage, sends one away with the thoughts "of things that thoughts but tenderly touch." What a thrilling suggestion it gives of our poor final dignity. You see the dying as they approach the end: they come crouching, haggard, stooped in weakness and fear; but at the sill they straighten, shakingly brave, to face that shut door. The man, more sullen or more fearful, still hangs his head. But the woman's face is lifted, and her hand is gently on his shoulder.

If one tries to be honest, he has to be cautious to note where genteel sentiment begins to slide into mere self-concern. After an hour or so of rambling, Père Lachaise begins to weigh on the mind, and crush the purest æsthetic. You are no longer, as the excellent phrase is, disinterested. That congregated mob of the dead is jumbled in an order as rigorously fantastic as names in an index. (Why should the man who invented gas-lighting have so much smaller a tomb than Napoleon's generals who adjoin him? But come to think of it, perhaps his real monument is in Lamb's essays.) You begin to feel an uneasiness, and speculate on the words *Concession à Perpétuité* cut in so many stones. Yes, you say, we must all concede to Perpetuity; but in the meantime, where shall we have lunch? If you feel the pricklings of self-pity, I think it sanative to pause on your way out to look at the grave of de Musset, the enchanting poet and wit who was so gorgeously sorry for himself. He asked to have a commiserating willow over his tomb; and I noticed that the growth of the tree has made it necessary to cut away part of the stone, removing one of his own poems that he wanted engraved there. There is a kind of hint in this. More loyal than the willow, his dear old sister sits chaired in stone just behind him, faithfully holding a volume of his poems in her lap.

Homer Croy
The Bathrooms of Versailles 1926

THEY came to a curve, turned into the widest, most beautiful boulevard Pike had ever seen, and there before them was the château of Versailles. Pike saw a huge, gray, dirty-looking building set on a hill surrounded by a high iron fence. Inside the high iron fence was a great bronze figure of a man on horseback. Later he was to find that it was Louis XIV, who had built the château. Pike was disappointed. Although he did not realize it until now, he had expected a grand, glittering palace flashing sunshine from a golden dome, for his idea of a palace was a compound of descriptions from the Bible and from motion picture scenes. Instead of such awe-inspiring brilliancy, here was an old gray, sprawling building, decayed and weather-worn. The courtyard was paved with rough cobblestones, and as he came closer the building had the sad, mournful look of a tottering man, once brilliant and powerful, but now grown old and useless, sadly waiting an end already too long delayed. But it still had glories — the amazing structure itself, the great arched windows, the huge cupids and flowers and symbolical figures chiseled high into the stone façade, glimpses of splendid stairways and the painted ceilings of magnificent rooms — just as an aged man might still wear his old and now meaningless medals, and raise worn, aristocratic hands on whose withered fingers costly rings, now too loose, turned, and which clinked feeble echoes of a past that would never return. Pike felt a distinct sense of disappointment.

But not so Mrs. Peters. Her mind was already made up.

"Isn't it wonderful!" she exclaimed.

"I wouldn't trade our state Capitol for it," said Pike.

"Why do you want to talk that way?" demanded Mrs. Peters. "You know it's a hundred times more wonderful," and she shamed him with a look.

"I was just saying what I actually thought," was all the poor man could answer.

A pack of guides and robbers selling binoculars, miniature reproductions of the château and figurines of Louis XIV descended upon them.

"Hell's huckleberry!" exclaimed Pike, "it's worse than a church booth at a street fair."

Selecting a guide, they bought admittance tickets and wandered from room to room in the great palace, staring at grisly ghosts of the dead.

The guide led them into a room half as big as their house in Clearwater, and pointed to the rare tapestries on the walls and to the paintings on the ceiling of cupids playing fiddles and whispering in the ears of naked women.

"This is the private bedchamber of Louis XIV," said the guide softly and reverently, as one must speak in the presence of the king. But Pike had no such reverence.

"I expect it was about the most used room on the place," he said.

"Pike," warned Mrs. Peters, "people are going to hear you."

"It didn't seem to bother *him*," he replied.

"And later," continued the guide, "it was the bedchamber of Louis XVI, and when the mob came for him he stood at this window looking down at them."

"Think of him living like this and the people starving to death! I think the old son-of-a-gun ought to had his head chopped off long before he did."

And again Mrs. Peters flashed him a warning signal.

"I don't care," he said; "it's what I think." He turned to the guide. "How many rooms was there in the palace?"

"One hundred and seventy-five."

"How many bathrooms?"

"One."

Pike's head went back and he laughed.

"How's that for you? And there ain't hardly a family in Clearwater that hasn't got a bathroom."

The Theater

The next place (which Bobby has near lost his
    heart in),
They call it the Playhouse — I think — of Saint
    Martin:
Quite charming — and *very* religious. What folly
To say that the French are not pious, dear Dolly,
When here one beholds, so correctly and rightly,
The Testament turn'd into melodrames nightly;
And, doubtless, so fond they're of scriptural
    facts,
They will soon get the Pentateuch up in five acts.
Here Daniel, in pantomime, bids bold defiance
To Nebuchadnezzar and all his stuff'd lions,
While pretty young Israelites dance round the
    Prophet,
In very thin clothing, and *but* little of it.
Here Begrand, who shines in this scriptural
    path,
As the lovely Susanna, without even a relic
Of drapery round her, comes out of the Bath
In a manner, that, Bob says, is quite *Eve-angelic!*
    — *Thomas Moore, 1818*

One is never hungry very long in Paris

⊷Cuisine

⊷*There is no food in Paris, only* cuisine. *Even the fast food is splendid, from the jelly-filled crepes on the streets to the* croques-monsieur *in the train stations to . . . well, not the McDonalds, perhaps, or the pizza. But why bother with them. Perhaps someone thinks even American food is exotic. Anyway, along with people-watching (on museum walls, in nightclubs, or simply from cafés),* cuisine *is the real draw in Paris. You may know by now where you should go and what you should order. But how, without fluency in French, can you manage to be treated like something more than just another faceless big-pockets or roast-beef? How can you impress the* maître d' *and his staff? A. Edward Newton shows you how to* make *your mark, while Bill Nye shows you how to* leave *your mark.*

A. Edward Newton
Dressing Your Own Salad 1930

PARIS is preëminently a city of restaurants: let it be said at once that none of them are as good as they used to be, and they never were. The Café de la Paix is still at the world's crossroads, but not so many people cross as formerly, nor are they so important or beautiful or wicked. Very well, so be it: I still prefer it to the Café Weber in the Rue Royal, "from which," writes someone, "you can get an excellent view of the columns of the Madeleine." But from a restaurant already too respectable I do not want a view of any church whatever. . . .

I suppose the most sophisticated man in all the world is the head waiter, or indeed any waiter, in a long-established restaurant in Paris. He can size up one to the nicety of a red hair: I would just as soon attempt to deceive God or my wife as a French waiter. But although one cannot deceive him, one can disgust him, by salting one's food before one has tasted it; and one can insult him by asking for Worcestershire sauce. One cannot get it, of course, or indeed any sauce out of a bottle, except perhaps at Prunier's.

On the other hand, if one feels up to it one can insist upon dressing one's salad oneself. It's an awful bore, and if one commits a single solecism one is lost, but if one gets away with it, it is like wearing that bit of red ribbon in one's buttonhole. It is done something like this. One must reject with disdain any sauce which may be supplied, and call for oil, vinegar, and the rest. These, when brought, must be waved away as totally unworthy. At this point it may be well to call for the head waiter. If sufficiently impressed, he will provide something from his own private stock, subsequently hovering to observe, assist, or silently condemn, as the case may be. Of the three or four brands of mustard provided, choose none, but ask for another; this will add at least three waiters to the interested audience now assembled behind one's chair, eager to offer advice. All ingredients being provided, you have but to mix them. There are two schools of salad mixing, one which demands an empty bowl to which the salad is eventually transferred, and one which does it all with a modest tablespoon — this last being unquestionably the greatest. One may further qualify by the gift of a tip which must be just right in amount, and one is morally certain of excellent attention and a nice table ever after at that particular restaurant, no matter how crowded it may be.

Bill Nye
A Parisian Soda Fountain 1878

I AM going to rest myself by writing a few pages in the language spoken in the United States, for I am tired of the infernal lingo of this God-forsaken country, and feel like talking in my own mother tongue and on some other subject than the Exposition. I have very foolishly tried to talk a little of this tongue-destroying French, but my teeth are so loose now that I am going to let them tighten up again before I try it any more.

Day before yesterday it was very warm, and I asked two or three friends to step into a big drug-store on the Rue de La Sitting Bull, to get a glass of soda. (I don't remember the names of these streets, so in some cases I give them Wyoming names.) I think the man who kept the place probably came from Canada. Most all the people in Paris are Canadians. He came forward, and had a slight attack of delirium tremens, and said:

"Ze vooly voo a la boomerang?"

I patted the soda fountain and said:

"No, not so bad as that, if you please. Just squeeze a little of your truck into a tumbler, and flavor it to suit the boys. As for myself, I will take about two fingers of bug-juice in mine to sweeten my breath."

But he didn't understand me. His parents had neglected his education, no doubt, and got him a job in a drug store. So I said:

"Look here, you frog-hunting, red-headed Communist, I will give you just five minutes to fix up my beverage, and if you will put a little tangle-foot into it I will pay you; otherwise I will pick up a pound weight and paralyze you. Now, you understand. Flavor it with spirituous frumenti, old rye, benzine — bay rum — anything! *Parley voo, e pluribus unum, sic semper go braugh!* Do you understand *that?*"

But he didn't understand it, so I had to kill him. I am having him stuffed. The taxidermist who is doing the job lives down on the Rue de la Crazy Woman's Fork. I think that is the name of the Rue that he lives on.

ఎ *The best guidebooks are those that tell you the name of the new out-of-the-way finds before, that is, all the other guidebooks do. It takes a great humorist like Robert Benchley to lead you to a place that will never be overwhelmed by tourists yet most perfectly embodies French gourmet ideals.*

Robert Benchley
The French They Are — 1936

I WAS talking the other day to my friend who happens to be a dachshund about this new restaurant in Paris where they cater exclusively to dogs. It is in the Champs Elysées, a very good location, he tells me, for a smart eating place.

"They call it *Au Colisée,*" he said, "although the significance of the name eludes me. I suppose that's the French of it. Hysterical exaggeration." (My friend comes from just outside Munich.)

"I suppose it's all right, if they want to do it," he continued, "but I see no reason for going sissy in it. Look at this!" He read from a menu which some German friend had sent him for his amusement.

"*La Patée de Bouky!* I'll give you ten guesses what *La Patée de Bouky* is. It's soup, rolls and potatoes! That's *La Patée de Bouky!*"

He then gave an imitation of an effeminate dog ordering *La Patée de Bouky*. He overdid it a little, but I got his point.

"Where I come from that dish would be called by a real name — *Kartoffelsuppe mit Brötchen*. There's a name you can get your teeth into! *La Patée de Bouky!* Faugh!"

"The French like to dress things up," I said.

"I don't mind their dressing up," he replied, "but they needn't make a drag out of it. Here's another! . . . *Le Régal de Nica*. Do you know what *Le Régal de Nica* is?"

"I'm sorry, I never tried it," I replied, almost dreading to hear.

"Le Régal de Nica turns out to be clear soup, new carrots, and meat ground up very fine. Now, there's a good, sensible dish, fit for any man to eat. But you can't go in and ask for *Le Régal de Nica*, now can you?"

"I don't suppose that French dogs mind it as much as you would," I said. "You have a different background."

"French dogs don't mind *any*thing, I have found out," he replied testily. "They even let people put fur pieces on them."

"I noticed you out with a sweater on the other day," I said.

"Oh, that old green thing!" he snorted, trying not to show his embarrassment. "I've had that six years. I used to play hockey in it in Germany."

"Hockey or no hockey, you appeared on the street in a sweater. All that I'm trying to prove is that you can't ever judge a man by what he has on."

"Maybe not," said my friend, turning back to his menu to change the subject. "But you can judge a man by what he orders in a restaurant. And I ask you if you would like to hear me ask a waiter for this *(looking up and down the card for something he had evidently been saving as a trump)* — here is it! *La Dessert de Nos Toutous!*"

"Toutous?" I asked, incredulously.

"I said *Toutous,*" he replied, sneering. "In case you don't know, *Toutou* is a pet name for a dog. It is equivalent to your 'bow-wow,' only less virile. I repeat — would you like to hear me go into a restaurant and order *Dessert de Nos Toutous?*"

"No, I wouldn't," I said shortly. He won.

We like to think of Parisian cuisine as an art, and it is one. Chefs study in the famous kitchens of Paris the same way dancers exercise at the bar and clowns tumble under the bigtop. But arts change. In drama, actors give way to scenery; in music, pianos give way to synthesizers; in comedy, well, feet keep giving way as they always have. Humorists love to talk about change. Like all of us, they are deathly afraid of it. But instead of turning their fears into the purchase of the latest gadget, they tend to look ahead and take progress to its illogical conclusion. Thus Alan Coren, editor of the venerable yet still youthful British weekly Punch, *considers how the recent pride of the French in their modernity might bring a delectable era to a tasteless demise.*

Alan Coren
C'est Magnifique, Mais
Ce N'est Pas La Guérison 1972

"Chère Vieille France! La bonne cuisine, les Folies-Bergère, le gay-Paris, la haute couture, le cognac, le champagne, les bordeaux! All that has ended. France no longer accepts that frivolous role. France is an industrial power!" *M. Pompidou, quoted in the Herald Tribune*

THEY showed him to the corner table, bowing.

"Ah, Le Tour d'Argent!" cried Mr. Sasu Yakahara, "I are hearing that this are best cooking in Western hemisphere! Crassical cuisine of highest order."

His host murmured, menus rustled, the waiters slid silently away. As silently, they slid back, plate-laden.

Mr. Yakahara put down his fork.

"This are interesting dish," he said. "How is made?"

"Quenelles de brochet faux," said his host, "is constructed from artificial pike. We tek an ordinary piece of coke, an extrude from eet ze silico-protein aggregate, weech is zen meexed wiz flavoured polyesterene an artificial colourings. After zat, we pass eet srough ze relevant moulding processes — five sousand biftek, ten sousand pike, par example, or four million snells."

"Snells?" said Mr. Yakahara.

"We mek ze shells from semi-extruded di-ferrous tinfoil," said his host. "Zey can be refilled up to feefty times per shell."

"Ah," said Mr. Yakahara, "so."

"Oui. We 'ave reduce unit-cost per metric ton to one-sousand-two-sirty yen."

"Yen?"

"Naturellement, ha, ha, ha!" His host shoved a magnum aside and plonked down a pocket calculator, upon which his deft fingers danced for a moment or two. "Wizzin six munce," he said, "we shall be ebble to ship ten sousand tons per week to ze Far East."

Mr. Yakahara reached, politely, for the magnum. He drank deep from his glass. He looked at it.

"I see," said his host, "you find ze 1972 Recycled Côte de la Seine Industrial Effluent interesting. Eet is, of course, mis en bouteille dans nos caves. Or, rathair, *sous* nos caves, ha, ha, ha!"

Mr. Yakahara put on his hat. He bowed.

"So sorry," he said, sadly.

It took him some time to reach the Boulevard St. Germain, hampered as he constantly was by men in berets waving patents, pulling alongside in electric cars, thrusting scale models of Concorde at him, and shouting logarithms and exchange rates at him through a fog of garlic; but he found, at last, what he was seeking, and walked inside.

"Welcome to Japanese Steak House," said the head waiter.

"Sukiyaki," cried Mr. Yakahara, without looking at the menu, "na-hai su mowaho ka-akha!"

"S'il vous plait, m'sieu", said the head waiter, "ah do not speak Japanese. No doubt, we can negotiate in Ingleesh, hein? Now, eef you will jus' step into our kitchen, ah sink you will be amaze' at ze new micro-wave oven mah company 'as develop wiz a view to . . ."

French and English

The French have taste in all they do,
Which we are quite without;
For Nature, that to them gave *goût*
To us gave only gout.
    — *Erskine, c1850*

OFF THEY DROVE IN THE CUSTODY OF THAT SINISTER-
LOOKING DRIVER

❧The Left Bank

❧ *The Left Bank of the River Seine is not only the center of the artistic and intellectual crowd, it's the site of everyone's personal Bohemia, where everyone dreams of going to school, meeting an artist or a grisette, and spending the rest of his life in one café or the other. No one has captured the true aura, the actual spirit and soul of Montparnasse, like Frank Sullivan, the one humorist courageous enough to tackle a city, yea even a myth, without ever leaving New York. And few foreigners have been able to capture the impressions of the Left Bank as well as the impressionistic writer Ford Madox Ford.*

Frank Sullivan
Dear Old Paris
Memories by One Who Has Never Been There But Has Heard and Read Plenty About It 1932

SEVERAL days ago I went up to the attic to get some moths for my new blue serge suit, and in going through an old trunk came across a faded velvet beret and a small reddish beard.

The beret and the beard I had worn in my student days in Paris! . . . I sat there for what seemed an hour — and, in fact, was an hour — lost in dreams of those dear, dead days.

Father had not wanted me to become an artist. He wanted me to join the business and learn it from the bottoms up. He was a brewer. I tried, but I couldn't do it. Milwaukee stifled me. I felt that there was something in me that was very precious that Milwaukee would kill unless I escaped. I knew I had to get away, or perish. I had to be free; free to live my own life in my own way, free to express myself. Father could not understand. There was a scene.

I left, and went to Paris. But Mother sent me plenty of money.

It seems ages ago that I dropped into the little *pension* in the Rue de la Paix, behind the Gare du Nord, off the Boulevard des Capucines, and bought that red beard. It cost but a franc. (Imagine getting a beard these days for a franc.) I remember Liane, the little *cocotte* who sold me the beard. She was my first love in Paris, a gay wisp of a girl, as affectionate as a puppy. We used to wander hand in hand, back and forth, over the Pont Neuf on spring nights when the air was soft with the wonderful softness the air has in spring in Paris.

I bought the beret at a quaint little shop in the Faubourg St.-Germain, just off the Rue St.-Honoré. A dear old Frenchman in a smock and wooden *sabots* kept the shop, but his daughter, Marie, a ravishing blonde, did most of the work. She was the fourth sweetheart of my student days in Paris. On a summer night when the air was soft with that marvelous softness the air has in Paris in summer, I would finish my painting, hurry over to the Rue St.-Honoré, and help Marie put up the shutters. Then we would leave *Maman* (as the French call their father) sitting in front of the shop, smoking his pipe contentedly, and we two would wander off, hand in hand. The old gentlemen would smile and wave at us with that tender understanding of young love which the French display so well whenever there is a sufficient *dot*.

Marie and I would go to Foyot's, in the Place Pigalle just off the "Boul' Mich'," for *escargots*. Gad, when I think of those *escargots* at Foyot's in the old days, prepared as only Pierre could pierre them, with that heavenly sauce that only he could conjure. Pierre could do things with a leek, some white wine, a bit of parsley, an onion, and a piece of old shoe leather, that you wouldn't believe possible. The sauce prepared, he would place it near the snails. Entranced by the magic concoction, they would troop out of their shells and pop one by one into the sauce, willing martyrs in the cause of good cuisine. *Et voilà!* There were your *escargots à la Pierre*.

Pierre's daughter, Diane, used to help him. I wonder what happened to that dainty, delightful minx who was the seventh love of my student days in Paris. On autumn evenings, when the air was soft with that divine softness of air in Paris in autumn, I would call at Foyot's for Diane.

"*Mais,* aren't you going to help me *avec les escargots ce soir, ma petite fille de joie?*" her father would inquire.

"*Enfer avec les escargots,*" Diane would retort gayly, and off we'd go to a little *bistro* called the Chat Rouge. No, it wasn't the Chat that was Rouge; it was the Moulin that was Rouge. The Chat was Noir, and it was on the Place de la Concorde, just behind the Madeleine (an *église*).

In those days only a few of us knew about the Chat Noir. George Moore used to come there, for one. He was a struggling young *concierge* at the time, or struggling *with* a young *concierge;* he told me which, but I have forgotten. Marcel Proust used to come there, too. A strange sort of chap, Proust. He was a neurotic, and an asthmatic to boot, and he would never leave his room. I shall never forget what an odd sight it was to see Proust come walking down the Boulevard des Italiens, in his room.

Of course, when I was studying in Paris, French cooking had not yet been invented by George Jean Nathan, but one could get perfectly good food at Napoleon's Tomb, which was run by a magnificent old rip named Margot. I can see her now — grizzled, bearded like a pard, fierce of eyebrow, keys jingling at her apron — taking her seat at the cash register and shouting *"Alors!"* at the harassed waiters.

Dear old Margot. She was like a father to me.

Matisse used to go to Margot's, also Matosse and Matasse and Matoose. I often saw Monet and Manet there, and Manit and Manot and Manou, and sometimes W.

And the singing we students used to perpetrate! *Mon Dieu,* it's a wonder our singing didn't bring on a second Terror. Our favorite was an old Provençal ballad called *"Samedi soir le bain,"* and if I remember correctly, it went like this:

Tais toi, mon bijou,
Tu sais que je t'aime,
Allons, dis donc, au Sorbonne!
Zut! Alors!

It used to make us cry, especially if we were homesick. Then there was another, called *"Peut-être,"* if I remember rightly:

Mon Petit choux,
J'adore vous;
Il n'y a pas des papillons?
Hein! Alors!

We sang that one when we were happy.

And such arguments as we students used to have, while the saucers piled higher and higher. We knew it all, or thought we did. How innocent, how naïve we really were, yet how furious we should have been if anyone had told us at the time that we were naïve or furious. The *vin rouge* wasn't potent enough for us Americans. We had to improve on it, greatly to the disgust of the French. We used to mix the *vin rouge* with *vin bleu* and drink the result, which was *vin pourpre*. But the French wouldn't drink the mixture. They used it for their fountain pens.

Fountain pens remind me of those Sundays at Versailles, watching the Fountains play. There were five of them, all accomplished musicians. There were the mother and father (piano and harp, respectively); a son who played the violoncello; another son, "Poodles," who supplied the comedy relief; and Louise Fountain, the daughter — dark, beautiful Louise, with such eyes! She played the B-flat cornet. Naturally, I was not long in making the acquaintance of Louise and the acquaintance quickly ripened into — ah, but one does not kiss and tell.

I shall never forget my first Quat'z' Arts ball. It was there I met Lucienne, the twenty-seventh sweetheart of my student days in Paris. A group of riotous, fun-loving students had stripped poor Lucienne of every last vestige of her costume. She didn't seem to mind awfully. I, *moi-même,* was no better off, a crowd of souvenir-hunting midinettes from Les Invalides having swept gayly over me, leaving me as bare as a tree after a visit from a swarm of locusts.

"Aren't you a mannequin in Worth's on the Rue Lamarck?" I asked Lucienne.

"Yes," she replied.

"I thought I recognized your face," I said. "It makes dawn. Will you drive out the Bois to Les Halles with me for some of that onion soup for which it is famous?"

"Oh, Monsieur is kind, but I am not dressed for onion soup."

"Nonsense, little goose," I told her. "Come just as you are." So off we went to Les Halles to watch the farmers and their oxen trudging in at the dawn laden with onion soup from the Hautes-Pyrénées, Normandy, and the Côte d'Azur. It was in December, and the air was soft with the entrancing softness of air in Paris in winter.

I recall the picnics at St.-Cloud — the funny, middle-class French families having their Sunday outing; husband, wife, children, mistress, all very gay. And Prunier's. I wonder if the chicken à la King à la Prunier's is still as good as it was. And the dear old Paris sewers — ah, but I ramble on until I grow tiresome.

They unveiled a bust of me at the Hall of Fame the other day. I looked about me at the eminent men who had gathered to honor the "greatest painter of the ages," as they were kind enough to term me. There were Dr. Nicholas Butler, Professor Irving Babbitt, Dr. John H. Finley, President Lowell, Edwin Arlington Robinson and a host of others. And as I looked about me, I became sad. The years had passed. Father was wrong and I was right. I had fame, wealth, honor; but, as I said to myself that day, what does it *mean* to me? Now that I've got it, what does it *mean* to me? Has it brought me happiness? I wondered.

And suddenly I thought that, with all due respect to Dr. Butler and all those eminent gentlemen, I would gladly give them all up for one hour of youth and happiness with Liane, or Marie, or Louise, or Diane, or any one of the two hundred and seventy-four sweethearts of that first rapturous year as a student in Paris!

Ford Madox Ford
The Left Bank Now and Then 1926

WHEN I was a boy the Left Bank was a yellow-purplish haze: to-day it is a vast sandy desert, like the Sahara. But immense! More immense than Europe, more immense than even Australia which, Australians tell me, is the largest continent in the world . . . Why I should have those two images I hardly know. Perhaps because in my boyhood the left bank was a distant city indeed, and from distant cities one sees at night in the sky a yellow-purplish glow; or perhaps because, now that I know the Left Bank better than any other portion of the surface of the globe, I have realised how minutely little one can know even of one street inhabited at all thickly by human beings. Or perhaps still more because I should find it less fatiguing to take the train from Paris to Constantinople than, at half past six in the evening when it is impossible to get a place in an omnibus or in any other type of vehicle, to have to walk, say, up to the rue du Bac from the Seine, along the Boulevard St Germain, past St Sulpice and so to anywhere on the Boulevard du Montparnasse . . . I am talking of course only of half past six when the spirits are low and vehicles unprocurable. I have as a matter of fact frequently walked quite buoyantly from the Ile St Louis to the Observatory and beyond at a time of day when taxicabs were plenty. But the impression of infinitely long walks with the legs feeling as if you dragged each step out of sands remains.

Are the girls in the Folies-Bergère really naked? Tourists often ask this question and guidebooks always skip it. We have gone to prodigious effort to find out the facts and pass on to the reader our investigator's full report. Full text of the report: "Well, yes and no."

❧Parisians

❧ *The principal sights in Paris are not necessarily made of stone or iron or canvas. And one need not always be running about viewing them. A pleasure as great as climbing the Eiffel Tower to view all of Paris stretched out below or walking the halls of the Louvre to see all of art's history spread along the walls is sitting at a sidewalk café watching all of Paris walk by.*

The Parisians you see are chic, charmant, à la mode; *they have* savoir faire, noblesse oblige, *and . . . But whom do we meet? Taxi drivers, bellboys,* maître d's, *bureaucrats. Rarely do we encounter the businessman, the artist (excepting the sidewalk variety), the manual laborer. Nor, unfortunately, do most humorists. But what they have to say about the taxi drivers and bureaucrats and hoteliers of Paris is worth listening to — or, at least, enjoyable. For those of you who may be too young to remember, Petroleum V. Nasby, the alias employed by David R. Locke, was one of the nineteenth century's great political humorists. Francis Steegmuller is an excellent storyteller and translator, from French, of course.*

Francis Steegmuller
The Foreigner 1935

IF it hadn't been raining as I came out of the cinema, I should have walked home: my apartment was nearby and the route anything but complicated — straight down the boulevard, crossing two streets and turning right on the third, the Rue de Grenelle, for about half a block. As it was, however, I hailed a taxi, and it was scarcely a moment before I realized that its driver, a ruddy-faced old man, was in the midst of an attack of perversity and nerves. "No! No!" I cried, as he started to turn up the *first* street, the Rue St. Dominique. "Two more blocks!" He muttered something, swung down the boulevard again, and then in a moment he was turning up the *second* street, the Rue Las Cases. "No! No!" I cried again. "The next one, please! The next street is mine! The Rue de Grenelle!" At this he turned around and gave me a baleful stare; then he spurted ahead, didn't turn up my street at all, and continued rapidly down the boulevard, as though forever. "But now you have passed it!" I cried. "You should have turned to the right, as I said! Please turn around, and drive up the Rue de Grenelle to Number 36."

To my horror, the old man made a noise like a snarl. Spinning his car around in a U turn on the slippery pavement, he speeded back, crossed the boulevard, and stopped at the corner of my street with a jerk. "Get out!" he almost screamed, his face crimson with rage. "Get out of my automobile at once! I refuse absolutely to drive you any further! Three times you have treated me like an idiot! Three times you have grossly insulted me! My automobile is not for foreigners, I tell you! Get out at once!"

"In this rain?" I cried, indignantly. "I shall do nothing of the kind. I did not insult you even once, Monsieur, let alone three times. You know quite well I did nothing but urge you, in vain, to drive me home. Now kindly do so. I shall give you a good *pourboire*," I added, more amiably, "and we shall take leave of each other in a friendly fashion."

He barely waited for me to finish. "Get out!" he cried. "Get out, I tell you! You have insulted me too often, and you will get out!"

I glanced at the rain. "Indeed I will not," I said.

His manner calmed ominously. "Either you will leave my taxi," he said in an even, hoarse tone, "or I shall drive you to the commissariat of police, where I shall demand the recompense due me for such insults as yours. Choose!"

"In such weather as this," I replied, "I have no choice. To the commissariat, by all means." And there we went.

The commissariat, only a few doors from mine, was not unfamiliar to me. I had been there several times before, on less quarrelsome matters, and as the driver and I entered the bare room side by side, the *commissaire,* sitting in lonely authority behind his desk, greeted me as an acquaintance. "Good afternoon, Monsieur," he said, calling me by name. "I can help you? What is it you wish?"

But the old man, to whom the *commissaire* had barely nodded, gave me no chance to speak. "It is I who wish!" he cried. "It is I who wish to complain against this foreigner! Three times he has treated me like an idiot, Monsieur! Three times he has insulted me grossly! I demand justice, Monsieur!"

The *commissaire* stared at him, his face expressionless; I felt that he, like me, was wondering in just what condition the old man was; then, turning to me, he asked me if I would have the kindness to make my deposition. He took up a pen, opened a large blank book, and as I spoke, took down my story in a flowing, plumy hand. The giving of my address to the driver, the two incorrect turns, the mutterings, the missing of my street, the rage, the ultimatum; all the *commissaire* inscribed imperishably in whatever the French call the Spencerian style; once or twice he interrupted me to reprimand the driver, who muttered beside me at various portions of my testimony. When I had finished, the *commissaire* continued to write for a moment, ended with a particularly fancy flourish, blotted his last line, and thanked me. Then he turned to the driver. "And now you," he said gruffly. "You depose, too, so that I may make up my mind on this perplexing question."

The old man, however, had no deposition to make. "Three times!" was still all he could say, in his thick, angry voice, gesticulating at the *commissaire* and glaring at me. "Three times, Monsieur! Three times treated like an idiot, and three times grossly insulted! By this foreigner! It is not to be borne, Monsieur!"

The *commissaire* looked up crossly from his notebook, where these accusations had been duly inscribed. "But the circumstances? Describe in detail what took place while you were with this gentleman. If the circumstances which he has related are not true," he said, casting me a glance of apology, "correct them."

But once again "Three times!" was all my accuser could say, and the *commissaire* laid down his pen rather briskly. "It is entirely clear," he said in a very definite voice, "that it is you, Monsieur, who are the injured party in this affair, and I shall be happy to indicate my decision by requiring this person to drive you to your door without charge. If Monsieur will now have the goodness to grant me the favor of a brief glance at his papers — a formality required by law in such cases as these — I shall dispose of the matter at once. Your *carte d'identité,* Monsieur, if you please."

Like a plummet, my heart sank. In my mind's eye I saw the desk in my study, and lying on it, forgotten, the identification card which foreign residents are required by French law to carry at all times. "Due to the penetrating rain, Monsieur," it hastily occurred to me as the only thing to say, "I have left my card at home, lest the moisture of the weather permeate it, and perhaps destroy it completely. In the morning I can easily bring it to you, Monsieur, and I hope that this will satisfy your requirements, which I realize are strict and necessary."

But I had done the unforgivable, and everything was changed and over with. "That will not satisfy the requirements," the *commissaire* said sternly, his face like stone. "It is true that you will bring your card here tomorrow morning, but in view of the present circumstance I am forced to alter my judgment in this affair. Due to the fact that it is raining, I shall request this gentleman to drive you to your door, but I shall require you to pay him not only for the entire journey from beginning to end but also for the time which he has lost by coming to this bureau. I assume, Monsieur," he said to the old man, "that you have left your meter running?"

The driver nodded, and the *commissaire* rose. "Then *au revoir,* Monsieurs," he said, unsmiling. "Monsieur will not forget tomorrow morning," and side by side, as we had entered, we left the commissariat. I had seen a gleam come into my accuser's eyes when the judgment had been reversed, but apart from that he had given no signs of triumph, and he continued to give none: he drove me home without a word. It was only when we arrived, and I handed him the exact fare, carefully counted out, that he spoke. "Monsieur has no doubt forgotten his promise of a good *pourboire,* that we might part in friendly fashion?" he said.

Petroleum V. Nasby
The Terror of the Streets 1882

WHEN an enlightened public sentiment drove the pirates from the high seas, and compelled them to seek other methods of supplying themselves with means for the enjoyment of luxury, I am convinced that every one of them came to Europe, and went into the hotel business. A few of them might have got hotels in America, but the vast majority came here. I did come across one at the Gorge de Triente, in Switzerland, who might not have been a pirate, or, if he was, he was either a mild one, or, being now very old, is endeavoring to patch up his old body for heaven. I am inclined to the belief that he was a pirate, but not of the sentimental order who shed human gore for the love of it; that when his schooner, the "Mary Jane," captured a prize, he only killed such of her crew as were necessary, in the action, and after the vessel had surrendered he did not make the survivors walk the plank for the amusement of his men, but mercifully set them adrift in an open boat, without water or provisions. That's the kind of pirate he was. And since he has been a landlord, he does not take every dollar you have — he leaves you enough to get to the next bank, where your letter of credit is available. I shall always remember this landlord. He is an ornament to his sex.

But the first hotel we encountered in Paris had for a landlord one who must have commanded the long, low, black schooner, "The Terror of the Seas," who never spared a prisoner, or gave quarter to anybody, but who hove overboard for the sharks every human being he captured, without reference to age, sex, or previous condition of servitude. Indeed, I think that after he was driven from the seas, he took a shy at highway robbery before taking his hotel in Paris, thus fitting himself thoroughly for his profession.

"Ze room will be ten francs, messieurs," was the remark of the polite villain who showed us our apartments.

"We, we," we cheerfully replied, for the room was worth it. We said "we, we," that the gentleman might know that we understood French, and that he need not unnecessarily strand himself upon the rocks of the English language.

But the next morning! The bill was made out, and as we glanced at it we forgave the English landlords — every one of them. Apartment ten francs, candles, or "bougies," as the barbarous French call them, two and one-half francs; attendance (we had not seen a servant), two and a half francs each, five francs. Then there were charges for liquors enough for Bloss, the American showman, not a particle of which had been ordered or had been brought to our room, and so on.

We expostulated, but when we commenced that, the clerk began to talk in French, and as all the French we had between us was "we, we," he had rather the advantage. In reply to some question he appeared to be asking, we said, "we, we," whereupon he dropped back into English promptly, and said that inasmuch as we admitted that the bill was right, why didn't we pay it? That "we, we" was our ruin.

"A little knowledge is a dangerous thing;
  Drink deep or taste not the Pierian spring."

Were we over with it? By no means. As we were ready to file down the stairs there came to our various rooms more porters than we ever supposed lived, each of whom seized a piece of baggage, when one might well have carried it all. We discovered, finally, what that meant. Those who did not carry baggage stood grinning in the passages, with their hands extended, and those who did expected each a franc. As we had passed the concierge, who had certainly been no earthly use to us, his hand was extended, and to crown the whole and have it lack nothing, a chambermaid came running to me with a handkerchief which "Monsieur had left in his room," and out went her hand. The brazen hussy had abstracted it from my valise, and held it till the last moment, that she might have some excuse for a gratuity.

We paid everybody and everything, and departed sadly. No matter how joyously you enter a French hotel, you walk out to the music, mentally, of the Dead March in Saul. But what are you going to do about it? You cannot sleep in the streets, and you must eat, and the pirates have you in an iron grip, and they realize the strength and impregnability of their position.

Beyond the — shall we call them "tourist people" with the same disdain they call us touristes? *No, let us not stoop to their level; let us wax philosophic and call them simply "them" — beyond them, you will discover Gay Paree, full of* esprit, *wearing its obsessions on its French cuffs, but hard to understand as the Mona Lisa, no matter how many so-called experts attempt a serious, profound examination. Here to help you get started are the great letter writer Lady Mary Wortley Montagu and the great humorist James Thurber.*

Lady Mary Wortley Montagu
The Stare and the Grin 1718

I HAVE been running about Paris at a strange rate with my sister, and strange sights have we seen. They are, at least, strange sights to me, for after having been accustomed to the gravity of the Turks, I can scarcely look with an easy and familiar aspect at the levity and agility of the airy phantoms that are dancing about me here, and I often think that I am at a puppet-shew amidst the representations of real life. I stare prodigiously, but nobody remarks it, for every body stares here; staring is à la mode — there is a stare of attention and *intérêt,* a stare of curiosity, a stare of expectation, a stare of surprise, and it would greatly amuse you to see what trifling objects excite all this staring. This staring would have rather a solemn kind of air, were it not alleviated by grinning, for at the end of a stare there comes always a grin, and very commonly the entrance of a gentleman or a lady into a room is accompanied with a grin, which is designed to express complacence and social pleasure, but really shews nothing more than a certain contortion of muscles that must make a stranger laugh really, as they laugh artificially. The French grin is equally remote from the cheerful serenity of a smile, and the cordial mirth of an honest English horse-laugh. . . . Does not King David say somewhere, that *Man walketh in a vain shew?* I think he does, and I am sure this is peculiarly true of the Frenchman — but he walks merrily and seems to enjoy the vision, and may he not therefore be esteemed more happy than many of our solid thinkers, whose brows are furrowed by deep reflection, and whose wisdom is so often clothed with a mistly mantle of spleen and vapours?

James Thurber
You Know How the French Are 1940

IT is touch and go (*il s'en faut de bien peu*) which is harder for an American in Europe to understand: the report of a cricket match in the *Daily Mail* or an account, anywhere, of what is going on in French political circles. On my two previous visits to France I never came close to understanding what was going on in French political circles (cricket I gave up long ago), so this time, before I sailed, I decided to buy some helpful books on the subject to read on the voyage over. I got Alexander Werth's "Which Way France?" (in spite of a title that sounded as if Mr. Werth wasn't very sure of what was going on himself); Mr. Gunther's "Inside Europe," which has several chapters on France; and a book on government by M. Léon Blum, written in French. This last, since I couldn't get anything out of it, I gave to a French steward on the *Ile-de-France* who turned out to be a Royalist and after that would not answer the bell when I rang for him.

Everybody in Paris, from messenger boys on up and down, is very politically minded and knows lots more than you and I do, or at any rate can talk much faster. I noticed the other day in the Parc Monceau, that loveliest of all green places, a small boy and girl playing Gaston Calmette and Mme. Caillaux, the principal figures in the notorious French political shooting of almost twenty-five years ago. All the little children in Paris play with toy pistols, but they don't play cops and robbers, they play editors and politicians. Now and again a frowning tot of five or six will toddle to a wall and with a piece of chalk mark on it *"Vive Maurras!"* or *"Les Soviets partout!"* or *"A bas les deux ans!"* or some other slogan of a timely political nature. It is somehow grimmer than the childish gangster hunts in our own parks and corner lots.

It is essential to know the names of a few French politicians when you are in France, if only to hold your own in the repartee and invective of the street. For example, if you refuse money to a French beggar, he is sure to shout after you that you are undoubtedly a member of whatever political party he suspects is trying to deliver France into the hands of her enemies. (All the political parties are trying to do that, I find in reading the various Paris papers.) In such a case all you have to do is shout back at your heckler the names of whatever politicians spring to mind: "Laval! Daladier! Flandin! Chéron!" Since all French party leaders are unpopular, even with their own followers, the names of any of them will serve very handily as epithets and are much stronger than pig, dog, cow, kind of sausage, name of a name, etc. If you are able to bandy the nicknames of the various politicians, so much the better. These nicknames form an important phase of public life in the French Republic and deserve a paragraph of their own.

Almost every one of the thirty daily papers in Paris has an editorial writer or two famous for thinking up nicknames for French politicians. Ridicule has for centuries been the strongest weapon of political assault in France (leading virulence by about half a head) and many a man has been ruined, I am told, by an adroitly bitter nickname, applied to him by some journalist or political opponent at the proper moment in his career. Once in a while the people as a whole apply the nickname (France is a race of wags), in which case the *malheureux* (the poor sap) is likely to be laughed out of public life in no time. Even if he survives, his dignity and importance are forever lessened. Take the case of M. Albert Lebrun. Shortly after he took office as President of France, he posed for the sound reels with his family, which included a tiny grandchild that began to cry as the cameras ground — and the sound apparatus recorded. M. Lebrun bounced the infant up and down on his knee, saying over and over again, for all France to hear, "Pooh, pooh—pooh, pooh" ("pooh" in French is *"pouh,"* but it's pronounced the same way). M. Lebrun has been known from that day, from one corner of the Republic to the other, as "Pooh Pooh." This name will stick to him forever. If he should ever form a cabinet, it would probably be pooh-poohed out of existence. What a day it would have been for France when Al Smith called Franklin Roosevelt "old potato" that time, had the two men been French politicians instead of American! The minor pleasantry was lost sight of in America in a few weeks, but a French political figure who had been called "old potato" would have gone to his grave as *"la vielle pomme de terre."*

The best way to meet a real Parisian is not to hop in a cab or try to talk politics; the best way is to fall in love. In fact, the Gay (as well as the Straight) Pareesian has made his city the symbol of not-so-brotherly love. The thousands of stories and films he and she have inspired form a veritable mythology of true romance, of suavité and sensualité. But don't look to humorists to fortify a myth; in that field they are definitely unilateralists (even when they talk out of both sides of their mouths). Here, on the subject of Parisian love, are Art Buchwald and the great collector of anecdotes Bennett Cerf.

Art Buchwald
A Matter of Pride 1957

PARIS is supposed to be a city of romance, but I wasn't quite sure why until I talked to three young girls who have lived in Paris for a few years. The girls, all foreigners, were comparing notes on Frenchmen, and it got so interesting I received permission to take a few notes of my own.

"Young Frenchmen," said one of the young ladies, "all have the same line. Suppose you are sitting alone at a sidewalk café, and a Frenchman sees you reading a foreign newspaper or book. First he will kick you in the heel or bump you 'accidentally.'

"Then he will say in French, 'Excuse me, Mademoiselle. I am so sorry. I hope I did not hurt you.' Then he looks under the table at your leg, not so much to see what damage he has done, but to see whether it's worth going on.

"If he thinks so, he says, 'I see you are a foreigner. What is your nationality?'

"If you say you are an American he says, 'Oh, America, I love America. I had a cousin who once visited Montreal and brought me back a present.'

"You say nothing.

"'How long have you been here?' he asks. 'Your French is excellent.' He says this even if you don't speak a word.

"If you reply, 'Six months or a year,' he brightens up. 'Then you must know Paris and the French very well.' The implication is 'Then you must know how we do things over here.'

" 'How long are you staying?' This is a very important question. If you say five years, he wants to forget the whole thing for fear of complications. If you say only a few months, he becomes tearful and sentimental. 'Oh, you're leaving so soon? How sad for me.'

"Then he wants to know what you're doing here. If you say you're a student, then you have a high priority. French boys feel that foreign girl students who can afford to study in France usually come from well-to-do families.

"The French boys also keep alive the legend that a foreign girl in Paris is bound to do things she wouldn't do at home.

"If you say you're a tourist, you get a low priority. A Frenchman considers a tourist an expensive item. And before there is a chance for a romance he has to take her to the Eiffel Tower, the Louvre, Notre Dame Cathedral, the Bateaux Mouches, Sacré Coeur, and the wax museum. By the time the tour is over, and just when the Frenchman, having invested his time and money, is about to make his move, a uniformed guide from Thomas Cook shows up at her hotel and whisks her off for the train to Venice."

"What happens if you say you are a student?" I asked.

"Then the Frenchman beams all over and says, 'Do you know Victor Hugo.' If you admit you do, he behaves as if you've both got a friend in common, and there is no reason for you to be strangers.

"When the preliminary questions are over the serious part of the interview takes place. 'Where do you live?' If you reply, 'With a French family,' his face falls. If you say, 'In the dormitory at the Cité Universitaire,' he also becomes depressed. But if you say, 'In a hotel in Montparnasse,' he smiles, takes your hand in his, and says, 'May I buy you a drink?' "

One of the other girls added, "The approach just described is usually made by students and young Frenchmen. An older Frenchman who can afford to ask you to dinner presents far more problems. A Frenchman will never ask you to have dinner with him. He'll ask you to spend an agreeable evening with him. Dinner, in his opinion, is only the first part of it. Although the French are supposed to be great gourmets, when they take a new girl out for dinner food is the farthest thing from their minds.

"During the meal they are constantly selling themselves, and the success they have with women.

"From there on the discussion goes on to where you will go after dinner. The only place he wants to go is to his apartment. If you say No, he gets very hurt and angry and says, 'But I thought it was agreed upon.' The discussion will continue at a sidewalk café until two in the morning. A Frenchman is willing to plead his case all night if you let him. If you still say No, he may become rude. If you're an American girl, he says, 'It's about time you American girls woke up.' If you are a Scandinavian girl, he will say, 'Then it's true, Scandinavian girls are as cold as stone.' If you're a German girl, he'll say, 'All you can think about is Germany,' and if you're a French girl he'll say, 'I know. You're saving your love for an American.' "

The third girl at the table said a Frenchman will never take a girl out more than three times unless he falls in love with her.

"He usually gives up after the first time, unless a friend he has met on the previous evening calls him the next day and says, 'Would you introduce me to that lovely girl you were with last night?' If this happens, he decides perhaps it's worth a second try. Only in rare cases will a rebuffed suitor go for the third time, and this time only for black coffee at a dingy sidewalk café."

"The most interesting thing about Frenchmen," the first girl said, "is if something happens between him and you, he pretends on your next meeting that nothing happened at all. But if nothing happened he pretends in front of his friends that everything happened. I guess it's a question of pride."

SOME DAYS LATER A FRENCHMAN STRIKES BACK

Dear Sir:

I was horrified to read in your paper about your conversation with three foreign girls who were discussing the attitudes of Frenchmen toward women. I think it is only fair to demand equal time to present our side of the picture. Otherwise this slander will be taken as fact and may make many attractive young ladies cancel their trips to our wonderful country.

It is true that the Frenchman considers himself an expert in the art of wooing a woman. But very few women I have come in contact with have complained about the treatment they have been accorded in Paris by Frenchmen, and if anything, we have sent women back to all parts of the world happier, wiser, and more contented than they ever were before.

Foreign women are naturally attracted to Frenchmen, because Frenchmen are naturally attracted to women. From a very early age we are taught that a woman is the most wonderful thing in the world, and a Frenchman's role is to please her in every way he can.

Anglo-Saxon and American women, who are not used to being treated as women, are suspicious of the attentions they receive from Frenchmen, but once they get over these suspicions they realize they have found a race of men who are passionately devoted to them, and are willing to devote their lives, even their money, to fulfilling every woman's dreams.

The description of a Frenchman trying to pick up a foreign girl in a sidewalk café could only have been described by an American girl. The Frenchmen behave in this manner only because it is expected of them.

A Frenchman would much rather say to a girl he is attracted to, "You are beautiful and I am in love with you and would you have a drink with me?"

But this approach would only frighten the young thing, and she might start screaming for the police. Therefore we are obligated to go through the boring formalities, not because we want to, but because the American way of life (and the English) demands it.

The Frenchman is penalized, not for the way he behaves, but for the way other nationalities behave toward their women. An American and an English girl (they are the outstanding examples) are taught at a very early age never to talk to strangers, and it's good advice in their own country, where men treat women with brutality and disrespect.

But in Latin countries a man is not being disrespectful when he talks to a strange girl. He is saying what is in his heart at the moment, and he is saying what he believes a woman wants to hear.

What the foreign girl does not understand is that a Frenchman is not discouraged by defeat as much as he pretends to be. His whole life has been one defeat after another, and if he brags about his triumphs it is only because they are so few and bring back such pleasant memories.

It is true that a Frenchman will discuss the problem with the young lady as long as she is willing to stay up, but he depends only on his verbal powers of persuasion and even if the evening comes to naught, he considers it a wonderful intellectual exercise.

The world owes a great debt to Frenchmen. If it weren't for Frenchmen there wouldn't be French perfumes, beautiful French clothes, and beautiful French women. French women will do anything to be attractive because they know Frenchmen care.

We Frenchmen have our faults, but not knowing how to treat women is not one of them. And I'm not talking about Brigitte Bardot.

Sincerely,

Count Artois de Buchwald.

Bennett Cerf
Sinsinnati 1956

AN heir to millions, native of Cincinnati, was dining alone in Paris when he thought he detected a "come hither" look in the eyes of the prettiest girl he had ever seen. "She jumped into a cab," he told his friends when he returned to America, "and I jumped into another. 'Follow that girl,' I commanded. Down the Champs Elysées we raced, across the Seine, and up the Boulevard Raspail. When she alighted at a studio building in the heart of the Left Bank, I was only a few steps behind her. I caught her on the landing of her apartment, and with a happy sigh I will never forget, she melted into my arms." "What happened after that?" his friends asked breathlessly. The excitement died down in the heir's voice. "After that," he admitted, "it was just like Cincinnati."

❧Tourists

❧*How you, that is, we, no, no, they, yes, they, but not the Parisian they, the us they, how they make fools of themselves! But consider what a burden they have to bear. They have to live up (or down) to the Parisian's expectations. Americans must be boisterous, on penalty of a dousing in the Seine. Britons must be proper, except at football matches. And Canadians, Canadians must be neither, and they must wield their maple leaves or no one will believe they're what they profess to be.*

Eliot Paul
Americans in Paris 1926

THE Americans in Paris, and they are becoming so numerous that I expect some political party in the States will soon start a move to permit them to vote by mail, fall into various classes and each class receives its share of abuse.

Those who have money excite the envy of the natives of low-exchange countries and the penniless have an especially hard time with their French creditors because of the current belief that all citizens of the land of the free are wealthy. If Americans talk, the sound of their voices drowns out the conversation of their more copiously be-vowelled neighbors, and if they keep silent they are suspected of plotting against European prosperity.

Those who know the French language have the disadvantage of being able to understand uncomplimentary remarks and those who do not are uncomfortable because they suspect such remarks are worse than they really are. If they are temperate or moral, it is called bigotry, and the other ninety per cent are thought to be disorderly. To conform to American customs as to dress and deportment exposes one to the charge of being provincial, and if one wears a pinchback suit, a black necktie, and drinks sweet aperitifs, one is accused of aping the Latins.

The tourists, whose orbit swings with reference to the Opera by day and Montmartre by night, ride the big busses, tiptoe through cathedral aisles, stumble along the corridors of the more accessible museums, infest the shops, motor to the battlefields, and spend the balance of their time looking for ham and eggs and ice-cream.

The hardy annuals who go in for society inhabit the Etoile district and are considered snobs by their countrymen and climbers by the remnants of the European aristocracy. The business and professional men have to prey largely upon the tourists, and while away their leisure hours during the closed season by listening to pep talks at the Chamber of Commerce or the American Club.

Visiting politicians entertain Paris journalists with their recollections of prohibition and prosperity in the States in exchange for hints as to what they shall tell the New York journalists about liquor and poverty in Europe, and divide the rest of their stay between the Folies-Bergères, the Embassy, the neighborhood florist, and the tomb of the Unknown Soldier.

The students occupy themselves in trying to find familiar books in the unindexed French libraries, in painting narrow streets in oils, bridges or gardens in water colors, making drawings and woodcuts of hoboes on the Seine, or practicing Czerny's School of Velocity on a pension piano. On Sunday evenings, they gather at some American welfare organization to look at the street scenes, etc., on the walls, and hear one of their classmates play Rachmaninoff's "C-sharp-minor Prelude," ending with community singing of "Seeing Nellie Home" and "Sur le pont d'Avignon."

On both sides of the Atlantic, the ways and days of the aforementioned groups are known. They have their friends and admirers, all except the tourists, and the articles or books written at their expense or in their behalf are either avowedly humorous or humorously earnest.

Owen Seaman
The Englishman on the French Stage c1900

When I'm in France, for Frenchmen's sake
    It is my rule to wear
What in their innocence they take
    To be a British air.

I like to feel, when our Allies
    My dress and manners scan,
That they can readily surmise,
    'There goes an Englishman.'

But since they never cross the wave
    To get the facts correct —
How Englishmen this side behave,
    What suitings we affect —

I have to imitate the type
    Dear to the Paris stage,
Hallowed by humorous mimes and ripe
    With immemorial age.

In chequered tweeds I go all day,
    Loud stockings on my legs;
And for my early *déjeuner*
    I order ham and eggs.

On cheeks habitually nude
    Red whiskers I emplace,
And make my frontal teeth protrude
    Some way outside my face.

A kodak and a bright-red guide
    In either arm I hug.
As down the boulevard's length I stride,
    Emitting blasts of plug.

My hobnails on the pavement ring;
    My brogues are caked with loam,
I read *The Daily Tale* — a thing
    I rarely do at home.

Strange slang and unfamiliar oaths
    My conversation spice;

I ask for what my body loathes —
    A morning tub of ice.

When *gardiens* lift their voices high
    Some trespass to condemn,
To their gesticulations I
    Oppose a perfect phlegm.

Enfin (in fine), when I'm in France
    I try my best to do
In every sort of circumstance
    What they expect me to.

It keeps the Entente fresh and hot
    To recognize in me
Its unimpaired ideal of what
    An Englishman should be.

Bel Esprit

*B*el Esprit is the goddess of the Parisians, more devoutly worshiped than beauty, wealth, dress, pictures, music, or anything else that can please this pleasure-loving people. And wo be unto the Frenchman or woman that enters society sensible of lacking the gift of tongues or, rather, the gift of a limber tongue. They had better see written over every portal, as over the gates of Dante's hell, *"Lascia ogni esperanza;"* for they may be assured they will be *lashed* in the purgatory of scorpion tongues within. . . .

At least half of the Parisian wit consists of ridicule. They laugh at one another as much as at everything else; but their ridicule is thoughtless rather than malicious, and it is amusing to see with what skill and tact they can pick one another to pieces, selecting at a glance the assailable points, and seeming to plant just the right kind of a shot in just the right place. — *W. Wright, 1857*

A WILD RIDE.

Engrossed in reading American "funnies"

THE PROVINCES

✣Transportation

✣No matter what they tell you there, Paris isn't France. It can't be; it has too many tourists. You've got to get out of Paris into what has given us the word provincial in order to discover who the French really are. After all, Parisians do vacation out there in the wasteland; they even stand for election there.

The first thing you will learn is that France is a very large country, almost exactly the total size of Rhode Island, Arkansas, Puerto Rico, Delaware, Connecticut, Hawaii, Washingtons D.C. and State, and, of course, the Show-Me State, Missouri. Most people cover all this territory either by train (the poor, gregarious, queasy, and chicken), by bus (the more impoverished, more gregarious, less queasy, and more courageous), or by car (the most wealthy, misanthropic, eupeptic, and courageous of all).

For the gregarious and faint of heart and stomach, trains are the ideal form of transportation: fast, sleek, modern, and public. The only problem you might encounter is the natives' horror of drafts, which has been most astutely studied by Albert Jay Nock in his tour of sites in the works of Rabelais: "Some authorities trace this superstition back to the medical practice of the Middle Ages; others relate it to the period of the tax on windows . . . The people in the other compartments seemed mostly to be well-to-do bourgeois, headed for the seashore where they would spend the whole day in the open air with practically nothing on. Here, however, fully clad, they shut tight every door and window at once, and began to loll and snooze and sweat and smell more and more infamously and intolerably hour by hour as the train went on, and were truly happy. There seemed a curious inconsistency in this."

But you're out to meet the French, not to pass judgment on their inconsistencies. Well, there's no easier place in France to meet people than on trains, no matter what class you choose.

Donald Ogden Stewart
Américains! 1926

MILDRED returned with an announcement.

"There isn't any drinking water in the car," she said.

Mrs. Haddock corroborated this.

Mr. Haddock took out a notebook and pencil.

"No water on train," he wrote, and after that he added, *"See about this Tuesday, sure."*

"There," he said, "that takes care of that," and he put the notebook back in his pocket with a happy smile

"But I'm thirsty," said little Mildred, "and there isn't any water."

"You forget, my dear," said Mr. Haddock, "that France is a *wine*-drinking country. We must try and adapt ourselves as soon as possible to French ways and French customs."

"Well, then," said little Mildred, "I think I shall drink some wine."

"You shall not," said Mrs. Haddock immediately.

"French children drink wine," said little Mildred.

"And eat frogs," added her mother, disapprovingly.

"I ate a frog once," said little Mildred, "and it made me very sick. First there was a terrible retching at my stomach and then —"

"If you please," objected the lady, "I would rather not hear about it."

"Why not?" asked little Mildred.

"Possibly, my dear," suggested Mr. Haddock, "the lady has a pet frog at home. How would you like it if some one ate Alice, your rabbit?"

"I'd love it," said little Mildred. "I don't like that rabbit. All she does is have little rabbits."

"Motherhood," said her father, "is a noble career." And he patted Mrs. Haddock proudly on the knee.

"Oh! Look!" cried little Mildred. "We're coming into a town."

The train slackened speed as it passed from roads to streets and from fields to houses. Old carts with old drivers waiting at crossings, with an occasional foreign-looking automobile and chauffeur in a white coat; narrow streets; walls; gardens; then more and more white stone houses; and finally the Hôtel de la Gare.

The train imperceptibly came to a rest in the station; the nice lady got up and left.

"Maybe this is Paris," said Mrs. Haddock, worried. "Will, maybe this is Paris!"

Mr. Haddock stuck his head out the window.

"I don't see the Eiffel Tower," he said.

"Isn't there some sort of a sign on the station?" asked his wife, becoming more and more nervous.

"There are several signs," replied Mr. Haddock, "and either this is the town of *Cabinets Gratuets* or *Chef de Gare* or *Sortie* — it's rather hard to tell which."

"*'Sortie'* means 'exit,'" said little Mildred.

"'Exit' is a funny name for a town," was Mrs. Haddock's comment.

"Sh-h-h, dear," cautioned Mr. Haddock, putting his finger to his lips. "We must not be too critical. Above everything else we want the French to like us and we don't want them to think that we are always comparing them with ourselves. Perhaps," he continued, observing on the platform outside ten or twelve members of the Legion of Honor excitedly discussing Racine, "it would even help if I grew a beard."

"You will do nothing of the kind," said Mrs. Haddock.

"But, my dear," said her husband, "think what a graceful gesture that would be. Think what it would accomplish in the way of cementing the friendly relations between Lafayette's country and ours!"

At that moment the compartment door was opened and a French lady dressed in black and carrying a small dog peered in.

Mr. Haddock smiled amiably.

The lady turned to her companion, shrugged, remarked, *"Améri-cains,"* closed the door and passed on down the aisle.

"I wonder how she knew," said Mr. Haddock.

As he spoke, the door was once more slid open and another French lady, also dressed in black and carrying a small dog, appeared.

Mr. Haddock stroked his figurative beard reflectively, and with a hasty glance at the window and a slight shrug remarked to his wife:

"Il est dangereux de se pencher au dehors."

"Américains," said the French lady and the door was once more slammed shut.

Mr. Haddock winced and looked at his watch.

"Lafayette is late," he said, and then he added, "This will make us kinder to the Rosenbergs when we get home, dear."

Christopher Morley
Wagon-Lits 1928

A VERY *tiny compartment in a French sleeping-car. At the back, door into the corridor of the car: Left, two berths, one above the other. Right, door into lavatory. Below it a small armchair. Just about room enough for two people to stand side by side. A large dinner bell is rung, off, and a voice is heard.*

CONDUCTOR: En voiture, messieursdames!

[*Enter at the back,* HENRY *and* KATHLEEN, *American tourists on their honeymoon, followed by a very villainous looking Swiss porter, in blue smock and heavily bearded, carrying luggage slung on a strap over his shoulder.*]

PORTER: Voilà, Monsieur.

HENRY: Thanks, I mean, mercy, mercy. Here. Quelque chose pour vous. [*Hands him money.*]

KATHLEEN: Oh, darling, isn't this *cunning!* Think of being in a French sleeper! What fun!

PORTER [*holding out money scornfully*]: Monsieur se trompe. L'argent français ne va pas en Suisse.

HENRY: What's he jabbering about? I gave him a whale of a tip. He's crazy. J'ai donné vous beaucoup, beaucoup.

KATHLEEN: Perhaps you gave him French money. We shouldn't have spent all the last of our Swiss money in that café.

HENRY: He can change it, can't he? Gosh, I can't remember everything. [*Gesticulates to porter.*] Beat it! Vous êtes riche.

PORTER: Madame, les valises étaient bien lourdes, Monsieur ne m'a donné que quelques sous —

HENRY: Oh, Hell! Enfer! Here, take all I've got. [*Gives him pocketful of small change.*]

PORTER: Bien, Monsieur. [*Exit.*]

[*Horn blown, off.*]

HENRY: Not much room, is there. I wonder if there is a club car where we can sit for a while. It's too early to go to bed.

KATHLEEN: It's like being in a bird-cage.

[*Door opens.* CONDUCTOR *puts his head in, and solemnly blows a little squawking instrument at them.*]

HENRY: Yes, and there's the parrot. — Have a cracker?

[CONDUCTOR *looks at them with dignity, and exits. The squawking sound is heard again outside.*]

HENRY: I suppose that means we're off.

[*Looks toward footlights as though peering through window.*] Yes, here we go.

KATHLEEN: I think it's marvellous how well you understand everything. Darling, you're *wonderful!* You really learned all your French in three weeks from the Doubleday advertisements?

HENRY: Sure. But I'm damned tired of scrambled eggs. Oofs broolay! That's the only food those ads tell you how to order.

KATHLEEN: Never mind, darling, some day a big French scrambled egg man will come to town. The boss won't be able to talk to him, and you'll take him out to dinner and close the contract.

HENRY: Where the deuce are we going to put these bags? They're too big to go under the berth. My God, travelling isn't what it's cracked up to be.

KATHLEEN: But think of being in a French sleeping-car on our honeymoon. Gee, I certainly am a lucky girl.

[*Low comedian, as sleeping-car attendant, opens door.*]

L.C.: Monsieurdame! Vous avez tout ce qu'il vous faut?

HENRY: What's he want? I wish they wouldn't talk so fast. Vous parley trop vite!

L.C. [*puzzled*]: Monsieur?

KATHLEEN: He probably wants a tip.

HENRY: I gave the other guy all my change. [*Gesticulates to L.C. to indicate that he has no money, turns out his trouser pockets.*]

KATHLEEN: Don't make him angry, darling. Suppose we were ill in the night. Here, I've got some. [*Gives L.C. money.*] Pour vous!

L.C.: Merci bien, Madame.

KATHLEEN: Ask him if there's any place where we can sit down awhile.

HENRY: Hum, Hey, Monsieur, vous avez club-car dans ce train?

L.C.: Monsieur?

HENRY: Gosh, he can't even understand French. — Une place où Madame peut — how the devil do you say sit down? — où Madame peut être comfortable?

L.C.: Mais si, mais si! Le double-V. Voilà, Monsieur. [*Points to door of lavatory.*]

HENRY: Dooblah-Vay?

L.C.: Oui, Monsieur.

KATHLEEN: I think he's talking about the — the bathroom. That's what the chambermaid at the hotel called it, doublah-vay.

L.C. [*delighted to be understood*]: Oui, Madame. Vous savez le doublah-vay appartient aux deux salons, ne laissez pas l'autre porte fermée.

HENRY: Yes, yes, the doublah-vay. Je comprong. Wee wee!

L.C. [*opening door of lavatory, explaining*]: Voyons, le monsieur dans l'autre coupé a aussi ses necessités naturelles, n'est-ce pas? Après faisant usage du cabinet, vous laisserez la serrure ouverte.

HENRY: He seems to want us to go in there. They're extraordinary, these people. Nous comprong, wee wee. Plus tard, plus tard.

L.C.: Bien, Monsieur. [*Exit.*]

KATHLEEN: I guess there's nothing to do but go to bed.

HENRY: We'll never be able to unpack those bags in here. If I open 'em I'll never get 'em shut again.

KATHLEEN: Let's go to bed as we are. Don't bother about nighties. *I* don't mind.

HENRY: Those berths look awfully small.

KATHLEEN: Never mind, darling. Think of it, in a few hours we'll be in France!!

HENRY: Yes, they must have some decent beds there. At least that's what I've always been told. [KATHLEEN *starts to undress.*] I'll go out in the passage; give you room to undress.

KATHLEEN: You won't be gone long, darling?

[HENRY *exits.* KATHLEEN *disrobes. Enter* CONDUCTOR.]

CONDUCTOR: Pardon, Madame. Il faut vous avertir que la visite de douane aura lieu a Bellegarde, vers minuit —

KATHLEEN: Go away! How dare you come in without knocking?

CONDUCTOR: Madame, la visite de douane —

KATHLEEN: Tell my husband. I don't understand.

CONDUCTOR: Ve visit you here; it is ze custom —

KATHLEEN: I don't like the custom. Go away!

[*Exit* CONDUCTOR. KATHLEEN *goes into lavatory. Voices heard, off.*]

CONDUCTOR: Pardon, Monsieur, mais c'est défendu de se stationner dans le couloir.

HENRY: Wee wee.

CONDUCTOR: Il ne faut pas fermer la porte, parce que la visite de douane —

HENRY: No comprong. Oofs broolay!

CONDUCTOR: I tell Madame, ve visit her in bed during ze night; it is ze French customs —

HENRY: It's a hell of a custom. Wee wee, wee wee.

[*Enter* HENRY. *Sees that* KATHLEEN *is not there, looks anxiously under berth, then taps at door of lavatory.*]

KATHLEEN [*within*]: Go away, you horrible creature! I'll tell my husband.

HENRY [*tenderly*]: All right, darling. This is Boydie.

KATHLEEN [*within*]: This is Teenie.

[HENRY *begins to undress.*]

KATHLEEN [*within*]: Darling, I haven't cleaned my teeth. I hope you won't mind. [*A pause.*] I'll be out in a moment, Boydie. Are you impatient? [KATHLEEN *emerges in her chemise.*] Oh darling! You were gone such a long time. [*Embraces.*] Oh, you frightened me so. I thought it was the conductor. He said he was going to visit me in the night.

HENRY: I'm damned if he will. [*Locks the door.*]

KATHLEEN: But that does sound as though we were getting near France, doesn't it. [*She gets into lower berth, he undresses.*] Boydie, do all Frenchmen have beards? Do you suppose their wives like it? — Oooh, it's awfully cold in these sheets without anything on.

HENRY: I don't suppose they grow them until they've been married quite a while.

KATHLEEN: Well, if I ever see you growing a beard I'll know what to think. My, this train goes fast, doesn't it? I'm just rattling around in this berth. I wish we hadn't drunk so much dinner. It's made me sleepy.

HENRY: I thought we might as well get rid of that Swiss money.

KATHLEEN: It seems such a waste of time to be sleeping on a trip like this. — Wouldn't the folks at home be surprised if they could see us now? What do you suppose they're doing?

HENRY: At the movies, most likely.

KATHLEEN: I wonder what's on at the Paramount this week? Oh, Boydie, wouldn't it be swell to be just going in to the Paramount, and then Roseland afterwards, and a stack of wheats at Childs! You know I don't think any of this wine they give you over here is near as good as a nice pineapple caramel soda.

HENRY [*climbs into upper berth*]: Maybe we can get a soda in Paris.

KATHLEEN: There was a new Harold Lloyd release announced that ought to crash through just about now.

HENRY: Yeah, but they won't get that over in this damn country for a hell of a long time. Gosh, it was terrible! All the pictures they were showing in Geneva were as old as mothballs. The only decent thing we saw on the whole trip was that Greta Garbo in Florence.

KATHLEEN: Yes, that was real cats. Was that United Artists?

HENRY: No *sir,* that was Metro-Goldwyn. If that bird Mussolini was a real statesman he'd tear down some of those old ruins and colosseums and build a real picture house. It's depressing to see so many old ruins about. It gives people a bad reaction; it hurts business.

KATHLEEN: Do you suppose the folks are really at the movies at this minute? There's a difference in time, isn't there? It's only about three o'clock in Bronxville.

HENRY: Sure, they're just getting ready to take in the afternoon show. — Well, I guess a fellow's got to travel sometimes; it opens up the mind.

KATHLEEN: Are you all right up there, darling? Your sheets aren't cold? Perhaps I ought to come up and warm them for you.

HENRY: I'm all right. I'm going to read this French time-table. It gives all the dope about crossing the frontier. I'm not going to let these frogs put anything over on me. [*Opens time-table booklet and begins to read.*] You know these French timetables are really a scream — "Among the baggages that may accompany the passenger into the compartment is a baby's bathtub."

KATHLEEN [*sleepily*]: It would have to be a very small baby. — Boydie, do you suppose we'll have a little baby some day?

HENRY: Not if we travel in trains like this.

KATHLEEN: Heavens, what's that?

[*A knocking on the door.*]

HENRY: Your friend the conductor, I suppose. Good Lord, you didn't encourage him, did you?

KATHLEEN: Don't pay any attention.

HENRY: It might be something important.

[*Leans out from his berth and unbolts door, which opens to reveal* 2D HEAVY, *as an anxious but very polite foreigner, bearded, in nightshirt and nightcap.*] Gosh, it's Santa Claus.

2D HEAVY: Pardon, Monsieur — Madame, je suis fâché de vous déranger mais vous m'avez fermé la porte, je ne peux pas visiter le cabinet —

HENRY: Listen — we don't want visitors. No visite, no visite.

2D HEAVY: Mais, mon Dieu, on ne peut pas passer par la porte —

KATHLEEN: Passport! He wants to see our passport!

HENRY: Oh, I get you, Steve. [2D HEAVY *tries to come into the compartment.*] Now, wait a minute; don't be in a hurry [*pushes him back*]. Where the devil did I put that damn thing? [*Leaps out of bunk, rummages in his clothes.*]

KATHLEEN: Boydie, it's in my purse. I'll get it. [*Starts to get out of bed, jumps back with a scream, remembering her attire.*] He's coming right in. Get out, you wicked old man!

2D HEAVY: Bêtise, tonnerre! Vous avez fermé la porte, la porte du cabinet, cabinet de toilette, lavabo, comprenez-vous?

HENRY [*showing passport*]: No comprong, no comprong. Here you are — passport, passport; all OK. Mr. and Mrs. Henry Nordic, Bronxville, N.Y.

2d HEAVY [*in despair*]: Gott, er ist verruckt. La porte du cabinet, fermé de mon côté.

HENRY: He's cuckoo. [*Imitates sound of cuckoo clock.*] Oofs broolay!

[*With a cry* 2D HEAVY *pushes past and rushes into the lavatory.*]

Oh, the good old doublah-vay. Well, that's what I call hospitality!

KATHLEEN: Oh, I'm afraid it's my fault. I locked the other door. You see, the bathroom belongs to both compartments.

HENRY: Good Lord! Well, live and learn. [*Locks both doors and returns to his berth. Reads aloud from timetable.*] "In view of avoiding all difficulty and all delay at the time of the passage at the frontiers, Sirs the Voyagers have interest to make to the agents of the customs declarations exact and complete of the contents of the baggages"! Say! Those Fatimas we bought in Geneva — where did we put them? [*No answer; he looks down from his berth and sees that she is asleep.*] Oh, well, the devil with it.

[*He turns out the light. After a moment's pause there is a heavy pounding on the door.*]

KATHLEEN: Judas, what is it now? [*Switches on the light.*] Don't let him in again. I shall have hysterics.

HENRY [*opening door a crack*]: What do you want? This isn't a comfort station.

[*Enter two customs officers in uniform.*]

1ST CUS: La visite de douane, Monsieur.

2D CUS: Vous n'avez rien à declarer?

HENRY [*pointing to door of lavatory*]: Dooblah-vay, dooblah-vay!

[*The officers look at each other, then open door of lavatory and look in suspiciously.*]

1ST CUS: Ce sont des étrangers. Américains?

HENRY: Wee wee. Mr. and Mrs. Henry Nordic, Bronxville, N. Y.

2D CUS: You 'ave nozzing to declare? No jewellery, precious stone, cigars, cigarettes?

HENRY: Wee wee — I mean No, not a darn thing, except about half a pack of Fatimas.

1ST CUS: You pardon, we make research.

[*Researches into the upper berth.*]

HENRY: Hey, stop tickling me. [*Leaps out of berth.*]

2D CUS: Madame, she remove herself also from ze bed so ve can pay tribute to her honesty?

[KATHLEEN, *modestly draping a blanket round her, emerges from the berth as they rummage in it.*]

1ST CUS: Mais, Madame, vous êtes charmante! Monsieur, you are ze
lucky man.

2D CUS: You may smoke ze liddle half-pack of Fatimas in honour of
so lofely wifemate. It is perhaps your first time in la France?

KATHLEEN: I think they're darlings! Is this really the frontier?

1ST CUS: Oui, certainement, Madame!

HENRY: Hot dog — I mean, oofs broolay!

KATHLEEN: Boydie, we're in France! [*She embraces* 1ST CUS]

CURTAIN

❧*Buses are like trains, but without all the formalities — in fact, formalities have been outlawed on French buses, as evidenced by the next selection — and without the rails that isolate the tourist from the infamous French driver, as experienced in the second selection.*

René Juta
Can You Cook Polenta? 1926

NEXT day, packed between brown corduroy and fierce mustachios
and a few stout ladies with black handkerchiefs tied round their
heads, I journeyed in a motor-bus to Sartène [in Corsica].

The bus was incredible. Everything was the matter with it, but its
two drivers who fought all the while seemed to understand its most
subtle whim. They dry fed it — from a petrol tin slung up on a strap
over the driver's head where it gently leaked itself away in futile
drops. A long tube connected the tin with the carburettor, which had
ceased to function in the usual way. To control the petrol flow it was
necessary that some one's thumb should remain pressed upon the
tubing. The drivers took turns in this tiring treatment. Also, at intervals, the tubing slipped and it became a gymnastic feat for one or
other driver to climb out and over the bonnet of the car while in
motion, and open the bonnet and refix the dry feeder and climb back
again.

Meanwhile, *all* the occupants took a verbal interest in the proceedings. It was dreadfully hot in spite of the fact that we were ascending
green slopes of fairly high mountain passes.

"Are you married?" said a brown-corduroyed giant next me, nudging up close.

This was such a surprise that I muttered that I didn't know . . . wasn't . . . was . . . no, wasn't.

"You are going, where?"

"To Bonifacio."

"To Bonifacio — alone?"

"To meet my brother." All the bus travelers were listening.

"Is he married?"

"No."

"That's good, for I have a sister who is not married. Will you marry me and your brother can marry my sister. And now will you say yes, because I am not poor and have good horses, and from my own country will drive you to Bonifacio, where I will ask your brother's permission to marry you."

The bus occupants who were his friends cheered loudly at this gallant suggestion, and became more interested, standing up to inspect me. No one seemed to find it odd. I replied that my brother expected me and would be disappointed if I did not arrive with the bus.

The corduroyed Corsican took refusal just as philosophically, but later he remarked:

"Can you cook polenta?"

"No," I replied.

"Ah, well," he said, "that's a pity — but even then my sister could have taught you."

His nudging arm lost some of its ardour with my more definite refusals, but he was determined that his country at least should impress me; also his knowledge of landmarks and the number of his friends: certainly every one we passed, whether bearded and riding a spirited Corsican pony, or driving a pair in harness a-jangle with bells, or younger friends perched on loaded motor-buses, postal buses, or aged ladies prodding goats from roadside pastures, one and all he hailed with a Corsican greeting.

He told me many things: that no Corsican tells anything on a Monday; that a weasel brings rain; that an ox bellowing means snow; that the shepherds tell the future in the shoulder blades of a goat; that the Church blesses the pigs before market, after a proper procession round the village; that when a child is born it is the husband who goes to bed for a few days' rest. And all of a sudden the bus stopped and he rose to his enormous height, took off his black hat, and said good-bye. As he walked down the village road, he turned.

"Will you change your mind?" he called.

Humbert Wolfe
Local Customs 1931

THE bus swept by incorrigible hair-pin bends to its lofty assigna-
tions in the Col d'Allos and the Col du Vars. The English on the
seat in front did everything to avoid looking about them, except play
bridge. For my part, I began almost to envy their desperate stupidity.
This return to the mountains was almost too much for a precon-
ceived attitude of permanent pessimism. "The boy that was born to
be king," the angry heart muttered, "and is ending as his own folly's
galley-slave." But the sweep of the oars could not be imagined, nor
yet the close confinement between decks. Here was all space — no
longer an attribute of the observing eye, but absolute. Snow and the
end of all barriers — how could a man be very deaf, very ill and very
disagreeable. At least he could be thoroughly surprised. With the
order imposed by a great railway company the P. L. M. bus hooted
religiously at each *tournant brusque*. Mountain-vehicles, on the
other hand, governed by a rigorous local etiquette, avoided this dem-
onstration, which to them no doubt savoured of a plainsman's timid-
ity. It should therefore have occasioned no astonishment when at a
bend about 6000 feet above sea-level, with a precipice of about that
height on the left-hand and a sheer rock-wall on the right, a huge
lorry, enormously loaded with barrels, crashed down upon the bus.
The incident was apparently an everyday one with both partici-
pants. The bus scraped the wall, the lorry inconceivably locked
without discharging either vehicle into the abyss. So they hung in
precarious embrace while the passengers descended and the drivers
exchanged fluent reminiscences. They had, it seemed, either
acquired or divined a most searching knowledge of each other's
affairs and, indeed, that of their families for several generations
back. It seemed as though the passengers were destined to wait
through time while this dual *Dunciad* ran its faultless course. But no!
round the corner puffed an object loaded with a huge crane. It had
not been summoned. Presumably it plied for hire, certain of custom.
With no haste, but with great efficiency the crane lifted the lorry,
swung it over the abyss and re-deposited it neatly on the road beyond
the bus. After full examination (and the taking of depositions from
all concerned with the assurance that the *procès* might easily be
heard within a year) the bus continued its impassive way to the Refuge of the Col du Vars. Here it seemed well to invite the possibly
shaken chauffeur to absorb a Marc de Bourgogne. This person,

strangely undisturbed either by the adventure or his oratorical exercise, agreed to accept the offer. "I understand," said I, "that the lorry did not hoot. That is no doubt the local custom. But might he not," I enquired tentatively, "have put on the brakes?" "O that!" replied the driver eagerly. "That was not his fault. He had, of course, no brakes."

The best way to see the French countryside, to visit vineyards and châteaux *and quaint little villages, is to drive yourself. But then the specter of the French motorist stares us in the face. Some of us dread the thought of jumping in a Renault and braving what appears to be an endless Le Mans, but others of us (or them) can't wait to try their skills and win the Grand Prix in a real-life video game. Believe it or not, there is à hazard on and off French roads that nearly rivals the French driver: the dreaded, three-headed (unless one's been cut off since this book went to press, in which case four-headed) French bureaucracy. The bureaucracy, children, and Robert Benchley's wonderfully bizarre sense of humor make his motor tour of France especially memorable. And for those who put the motor before the tour, there's Stephen Leacock's John Gasoline Smith to show you the way.*

Robert Benchley
Route Nationale 14
How to Motor from Cherbourg to Antibes
via Cherbourg 1930s

COME with me and we will motor through Sunny France, from the tippity-tip of Cherbourg to the top-*tip*pity-tip of Cap d'Antibes! Or come with me and we will go over to Dinty Moore's on Forty-sixth Street for some spareribs and sauerkraut. Anyway, we'll do *some*thing!

If it's motoring through France we're going, we shall have to get started earlier. We shall also have to have a motor. Perhaps we had better decide right now on Dinty Moore's.

To motor pleasantly from Cherbourg to Antibes, it is preferable to use one's own car, as in a rented French limousine the driver's mustache is always too big and too black. There really isn't much worry involved in taking your own car, unless you happen to be watching while they are lowering it down from the ship to the tender. Furthermore, in your own car, you don't care so much what the children do to the back seat.

THE ARRIVAL

On arriving at the port of Cherbourg you are met on the tender by a representative of the A.A.A. who will tell you that your license-plates have just barely not arrived yet, but that they will be in tomorrow *très de bonne heure* (along about noon). So this means spending the first night of your motoring trip in Cherbourg (Grand Hotel du Casino, or behind the barrels on the new pier). Anywhere you stay, you get to know Cherbourg.

While roaming the streets of this quaint old seaport town (Napolean said of it: *"J'avais résolu de rénouveller à Cherbourg les merveilles de l'Egypte,"* but he didn't quite make it, doubtless due to the lack of Egyptians), one can see much that is of interest — to the Cherbourgians. One may also *be* seen and pointed out as a native by the boat-train passengers as they roll slowly through the Main Street. ("Look, Harry," they say, "at those picturesque old natives! Don't those people *ever* bathe, do you suppose?") One can also get a line on the boat-train passengers themselves from the outside. They don't shape up so hot, either. (Beauty note: Every woman looking out at the windows of the incoming boat-train has just been freshly lipsticked in preparation for embarkation.)

A good place to spend the evening while waiting in Cherbourg is not the Café de Paris across the bridge. It isn't much fun in the Grand Hotel du Casino, either. But you are all excitement at the prospect of your early start in the morning, so it's early to bed, after a chat with the quaint old negro concierge from Philadelphia, Pa.

At seven o'clock you are up and ready, with everything strapped on the car and the children buried in the back seat under the extra hampers and coats. (One child is buried so deeply that he is a great big boy by the time he is remembered and dug out.) The maps are spread open and a schedule arranged which calls for lunch at Lisieux. (Hotel France et Espagne. Bad Martinis.) A light rain is falling.

At the *mairie* it will be found that the license-plates have not yet come, and eighteen shoulders will be shrugged. The car will then be driven back to the hotel (Grand Hotel du Casino, 100 fr.) and a more thorough tour made of

CHERBOURG (¼ kms.). A quaint seaport town, of which Napoleon once said: *"J'avais résolu de rénouveller à Cherbourg les merveilles de l'Egypte."* It was his intention to revive in Cherbourg the marvels of Egypt is the way it looks. You may see a statue of

Napoleon in the public square across the bridge. On the other hand, you may not. You may also see Pauline Frederick in "The Woman Thou Gavest Me," the film for which was found in an old bureau drawer by the exhibitor. Then there is always the Café de Paris. And the Grand Hotel du Casino.

The license-plates not having come at fifteen o'clock, it is decided to spend the night in

CHERBOURG (¼ kms.). A quaint seaport town which Napoleon once designated as the place where he was to revive the marvels of Egypt. To this end he appointed Vauban, the great engineer, to construct fortifications and plan a harbor which should be impregnable. (You learn a little more each day you stay in Cherbourg. By the time I left I was being groomed as Opposition candidate for Mayor. I was letter-perfect in the opposition, but my age was against me.)

During the second evening in Cherbourg, after seeing that everything is going all right at the Café de Paris, you can read up on the rules of the road, some of the most readable being:

1. In France one keeps to the right, except when skidding.

2. Danger signals along the road are represented by black triangles with little pictures on them. Be careful not to become so interested in looking at the pictures that you forget the danger. A picture of two little hills side by side (these French!) means *cassis,* or a gully across the road (Cassis, in vermouth form, also makes a nice gully across the road if taken in sufficient quantities). A cute little gate means a *passage à niveau gardé* or protected level crossing. An even cuter choo-choo (if you are traveling with children), with smoke and everything, means an unprotected level crossing. This is the one you mustn't get too fascinated by.

3. The way to say "dust clip of front hub" is *"ressort cache poussière de moyeu avant,"* something you really don't have to learn as you can always point. In case you end up in Holland the way to say it is *"Sluitveerje der smeeropening,"* which is just plain silly.

4. Gasoline is sold by the *bidon.* Be careful about this.

5. An automobile tourist arriving in France on March first for a four months' visit will take out a *laissez-passer* for thirty days. This immediately puts the tourist under suspicion in the eyes of all officials and sometimes ends in his incarceration.

By this time it is bedtime, as you have to make an early start in the morning. There are very tall hat-racks in each bedroom of the Grand Hotel du Casino, from which you may hang yourself if you have to stay a third day in Cherbourg.

Up at seven, in a light rain. A chat with the colored concierge from

Philadelphia, one last look around at the Café de Paris, a visit to Napoleon's monument to make sure what it was he hoped to make out of Cherbourg, and, at eleven o'clock sharp a trip to the *mairie* where there is tremendous excitement owing to the arrival of the license-plates. By this time you have made such friends with everyone in the place, including the Mayor, that it costs you three hundred francs in tips. The adjusting of the plates, the signing of the Peace Treaty, the shaking hands and the shaking-down, take an hour and a half, so it is decided to have lunch at the

GRAND HOTEL DU CASINO (35 fr.). A quaint old hostelry situated hard by the *quai* overlooking the harbor fortifications built for Napoleon by Vauban, the great engineer.

THE START

Leaving Cherbourg, believe it or not, we ascend a gentle grade along the winding roads through picturesque Normandy (light rain). The excitement of actually riding in a moving automobile proves too much for the children and a stop has to be made just this side of

BAYEUX, famous for its tapestry and cathedral, neither of which we see. The excitement of passing through a French town other than Cherbourg is too much for the children and another stop has to be made just the other side of

BAYEUX, famous for its tapestry and cathedral, although there was a perfectly good hotel (Hotel de Luxembourg) on the way through. At this point it is discovered that the "funnies," bought in an American newspaper the day before in Cherbourg, have been packed in a suitcase on the trunk rack, necessitating taking the car apart to get them. From here on the children are engrossed in reading American "funnies," which gives us quite a stretch without a stop to

CAEN (pronounced "Kong"), famous as being the first train-stop from Cherbourg to Paris, where most American tourists think they are in Cayenne.

Stop for the night at LISIEUX (scheduled for lunch the day before). Hotel Franc et Espagne. (Bad Martinis.) The residents of Lisieux sleep all day in order to be abroad all night under the windows of the Hotel France et Espagne (under the window of Room 34 in particular), where they walk up and down in an especially whittled type of sabot, pinching children to make them cry. Some also carry small horns or attach even smaller ones to bicycles, thereby effecting a squeak in synchronization with the bicycle wheels. This causes the fox terriers (an exceptionally repulsive breed, fat and soiled) to bark, which, in turn, causes the children to cry.

Up at four (bad Martinis) and on the road at five-thirty, passing through such interesting towns as Évreux, Mantes, Flins, and St. Germain-en-Laye, none of which are seen owing to the entire family catching up on last night's sleep.

We are awakened by the sound of heavy traffic and, on inquiring where we are, are told that we are in Paris (Porte Maillot).

Here ends the first stage of our automobile tour from Cherbourg to Antibes. The stay in Paris is regulated by the length of time it takes to recover the use of our limbs and have the *ressort cache poussière de moyeu avant* fixed. The number of remaining checks in the A.B.A. book has also something to do with it.

CONTINUATION OF TOUR
(Paris to Antibes)

The P.L.M. train (*Wagon Lits*) leaves Paris (Gare de Lyons) at 19:40, arriving at Cannes at 11:02 the next day. Fifteen minutes motor trip to Cap d'Antibes.

Stephen Leacock
Travel Is So Broadening 1929

I

THE IDEAL MOTOR TRIP IN EUROPE

"No more wonderful revolution in travel and in the culture that travel alone can bring has ever been effected than that occasioned by the advent of the motor-car." So writes the enthusiastic and eloquent author of an automobile guide for foreign travel.

"Not only," continues the writer, "does it bring within our eye a wonderful panorama of scenery, but it enables the fortunate traveler to envisage in his rapid flight the great epochs of history, to follow in the footsteps of Charlemagne and Hannibal, to gaze with awe on the silent dungeons of the middle ages and the crumbling amphitheatres of Roman Gaul.

"We set our course, let us say, down the valley of the Rhône. Here, at the very outset, is a massive and impressive scenery. For many miles of it, not even the new world of America can offer such a prospect of waving forests, whose age-old trees echoed to the hunting horns of the Merovingian Kings and of dark gorges cleft deep into river valleys by uncounted centuries of time. Here again we are out in the open, smiling country, a land of vineyards basking in the sun, of little roadside inns where red wine is poured out for us from stone jugs and where the luscious fruit of Provence is heaped in a very cornucopia on the table. Our noon-day halt is at Nîmes, where the great Roman amphitheatre, half in ruins, rears its sunlit, stone benches to recall the gladiatorial combats of the great days of the empire. Here sat, perhaps, a Nero or a Trajan, under a sweeping canopy of royal purple that rustled in the summer sun, while all about him stormy shouts of savage joy greeted the death throes of a defeated gladiator.

"A little further on in our journey and here is Avignon, the medieval city of the popes, and Carcassonne, whose lofty turrets recall the splendors and the mysteries of the Middle Ages. . . ."

And so forth. . . .

II

THE REAL THING

Now let us put beside this the real vacation tour in a motor through Europe. We take it from the text of letter No. 13 from the correspondence of John Gasoline Smith, motorist-on-the-move, three days out from Paris and heading southward, westward, and a little east.

"On Thursday we got away to a good start from the town where we had slept and hit it up to about forty to forty-two an hour from 6.30 to 7.43, taking on gas only at the start, and filling up with twenty gallons. We calculate that in this country, which is hilly and rough, though the roads are good, we can't get more than twelve out of a gallon. In the flat country, just out of Paris, we could easily get fourteen. The traction lift and the extra friction on the big hills makes a lot of difference. The wife and I find it mighty interesting to keep the figures and compare how many miles you can get out of a gallon in different parts of France. It gives a sort of diversity to the trip. In fact, we find that if you keep tab on your gasoline and your oil, and make a table of your mileage and figure out your day's run in sections, it lends a great interest to the trip and prevents it from being monotonous.

"In France you soon learn the dodge of filling your tank right up, because at each station you are supposed to tip the man, and the tip is the same anyway. But we don't mind the little stops anyway, because in France there is always something to study and look at, such as the way they set up their gas tanks, not a bit like ours and with a slower feed, and the much longer flexible pipe they use, so that you don't need to drive off the road at all to get gas at the station.

"As I said to Lil, it is only when you travel that you really learn about a country. If we hadn't taken this trip, I would never have known that in France they use a much more volatile gas than we do. It suits the climate better; and certainly the French climate is beautiful, with no danger of freezing up your radiator. In the French climate your oil never gets thick, but always runs nice and free and gets right to your bearings.

"Naturally, we are both picking up a lot of French, and can manage anything we want, such as, 'Aves-vous de la gasoline?' or 'Combien chargez-vous pour gasoline ce matin?' and 'Voulez-vous avoir la bonté s'il vous plaît de me donner un coup d'eau dans le radiator?' and all the common, ordinary things like that.

"Coming down the valley of the big river here, which is called the Rhône, though at home we always heard of it as the Rhine, we struck quite a lot of bush and mountain country. But it didn't matter, because the roads are all stone roads and the sight line is good, so that all you have to do is keep your eye on the road and go straight ahead.

"We made nearly 200 miles before lunch in spite of being held up for fifteen minutes by an old Roman town (the book said it was Roman), where the paving was so atrocious that we had two or three times to back out of a street again after getting started in it. However, we are getting wise to the game, and we find that when once you understand travel here you can avoid all the old towns by making a detour. Even if it takes you a few miles out of your direct way, it is well worth it.

"We got badly fooled, though, at a place called Nim, or Neam, or something like that, where we decided not to make a detour because we wanted to have a look at what we thought was a big new football stadium. It lost us about twenty-five minutes of our time and in the end the laugh was on us, because when we got nearer we saw it wasn't a stadium at all, but just some sort of old ruin. We managed to avoid it before we got too close.

"We had lunch at a gasoline station. And then we got away on a clear stretch, and before the end of the day we had actually done 400 miles.

"We are reckoning that if we can do, say 250 miles a day from here, we can get clear to Spain by Thursday. I was suggesting to Lil that perhaps we could do better if we made a good part of our run after dark, when it's cooler. There's not much traffic in France after dark, and with good lights on your car you can see the road as clear as day, and that's all you need to see.

"We are both fascinated with the trip and want very much to come again, if I can get away, and go over this same ground in winter. I'd like to see how the consumption of gasoline would compare in the colder weather. I've got an idea that the per mile cost of gasoline in France per ton of distance is away more than at home. It's hard to reckon it out, as all the measurements are different. But I keep figuring on it in my head as we drive along.

"That's another great thing about travel in Europe. It helps you to reflect. Often I fall into a regular reverie about it, and only wake up to hear a man saying, 'Combien de gasoline, Monsieur?' That's the French for, 'How much gasoline, boss?'"

☙ *There* is *a positive side to driving: freedom and, most of all, adventure, even, as with Mark Twain, when you hire a driver (don't be picky and point out that, for the most part, Twain predated the automobile; what's a few horsepower to a friend, especially when the drivers never change).*

Mark Twain
The King of Drivers 1880

WE made the tramp from Martigny of Argentière in eight hours. We beat all the mules and wagons; we didn't usually do that. We hired a sort of open baggage-wagon for the trip down the valley to Chamonix, and then devoted an hour to dining. This gave the driver time to get drunk. He had a friend with him, and this friend also had time to get drunk.

When we drove off, the driver said all the tourists had arrived and gone by while we were at dinner; "but," said he, impressively, "be not disturbed by that — remain tranquil — give yourselves no uneasiness — Their dust rises far before us, you shall see it fade and disappear far behind us — rest you tranquil, leave all to me — I am the king of drivers. Behold!"

Down came his whip, and away we clattered. I never had such a shaking up in my life. The recent rains had washed the road clear away in places, but we never stopped, we never slowed down, for anything. We tore right along, over rocks, rubbish, gullies, open fields — sometimes with one or two wheels on the ground, but generally with none. Every now and then that calm, good-natured madman would bend a majestic look over his shoulder at us and say, "Ah, you perceive? It is as I have said — I am the king of drivers."

Every time we just missed going to destruction, he would say, with tranquil happiness, "Enjoy it, gentlemen, it is very rare, it is very unusual — it is given to few to ride with the king of drivers — and observe, it is as I have said, *I* am he."

He spoke in French, and punctuated with hiccups. His friend was French, too, but spoke in German — using the same system of punctuation, however. The friend called himself the "Captain of Mont Blanc," and wanted us to make the ascent with him. He said he made more ascents than any other man, — 47, — and his brother had made 37. His brother was the best guide in the world, except himself — but he, yes, observe him well, — he was the "Captain of Mont Blanc" — that title belonged to none other.

The "king" was as good as his word — he overtook that long procession of tourists and went by it like a hurricane. The result was that we got choicer rooms at the hotel in Chamonix than we should have done if his majesty had been a slower artist — or rather, if he hadn't most providentially got drunk before he left Argentière.

The irreducible minimum known as the rasurel.

❧Sightseeing

❧*No guidebook worth its weight in gifts no one will ever wear or use or even put on a shelf can ignore the myriad sights of the provinces, its fields and forests, its churches and walled towns, its caves and mountains, its histories and tales. Therefore, The Humorists' Guide provides you with a whirlwind, counterclockwise, complete and unexpurgated tour of France, beginning in Normandy. Your guides include such wise and weathered travelers as Petroleum V. Nasby, Melville Chater, Jan and Cora Gordon, Margaret Fishback, Charles Dickens, Tibor Koeves, S. J. Perelman, and Harriet Beecher Stowe.*

Petroleum V. Nasby
Normandy: A Sermon
on Cathedrals 1882

AFTER a light lunch in an arbor in a delicious garden back of a café, we started to see Rouen, its cathedral and the statue of Joan, and what else was to be seen. We urged Tibbitts to accompany us. He concluded to do it, though he protested it was far more pleasant to sit in that arbor, even though it was beastly wine he was drinking instead of the delicious whisky of Oshkosh, than it was tramping around in search of antiquities.

We came to a narrow street, one of the kind only to be seen in French cities. The entire space from wall to wall could not have been twelve feet, and on either hand were curious houses, seven stories high, entered by dark, narrow tunnels rather than passages, but with flowers at every window, clear to the queer, quaint top, which was continued after it had reached what should have been its summit. The professor stopped before one of these dark passages, and observed a parcel of illy dressed but marvelously clean children — there are no dirty children in France — playing some game.

"It is wonderful!" said the Professor, in an ecstacy; "here are we, of the new West, standing on ground in a street through which, may be, the soldiers of old France marched. Here are we within sight of the place where Joan of Arc was burned, on ground pressed by the feet of Charlemagne. In this house, perchance, were born heroes; within these walls for hundreds of years have been born children who have grown to manhood, and died. These children, playing in this gutter, were born in this historic city, and —"

"And they all speak French," interrupted Tibbitts, "which I can't, but, thank Heaven, I can lay all over 'em in English. Look here, Professor, don't give us any more rot about this being old. We are just as old in Oshkosh as they are in Rouen. When the old Norman warriors were cruising about loaded down with pot-metal, killing each other, the Indians of America were doing the same thing among themselves, only they were clothed more sensibly. A breech clout was a thundering sight more comfortable in the summer than steel armor, and I don't know that killing a man with a lance was any more deserving of adoration than killing one with a bow and arrow. The point to it all is killing the man. Antiquity! What do you know about it? Here is a lot of stone that has been piled up a thousand years or more. How do you know but what the Indians are older than the Gauls? I hold that they are. The Gauls built a cathedral that is standing yet. I defy you to go anywhere in Wisconsin and find such a cathedral standing. What does that prove? Why! that the ancient Indians built their cathedrals so much farther back than the Gauls that they have all disappeared. Nothing can resist the iron tooth of time. Now I think that this cathedral is rather modern than otherwise. [By this time we were in front of the cathedral.] It is tolerably ancient, but if you want to visit a really old country, go to Wisconsin. That is so old that everything of this kind has disappeared entirely."

Melville Chater
Brittany: A Heathen
Father's Fable 1932

WE came to Redon, where we were halted by a broken lock and a consequent tie-up of navigation. Another of Brittany's apparently modern towns, which are in fact of such ancient origin, Redon derives its name from a Celtic tribe, the Redones, and neighbors in Carnac, the so-called Stonehenge of Brittany, some of the greatest of Celtic remains.

Strangely impressive, as you approach sea-facing Carnac, is the spectacle of those gigantic menhirs, or standing stones, which stretch in multiple parallel lines across five miles of wild moorland. The wind moans timelessly up their alleys, the wheeling gull looks down upon their solitary remoteness. Yet those bleak spaces must once have teemed with human activities, since nearly 300 groups of such monuments exist within a seven-mile radius of Carnac, which itself contains some 3000 menhirs. And the considerable resourcefulness of the stone-using Celts, in addition to agriculture, is apparent in that regional menhirs weigh up to 375 tons, and that some of their alignments are so oriented as to suggest a rudimentary means of establishing the winter and summer solstices — in fact, a neolithic calendar that would have been accurate about 1600 B.C.

Whatever motivated the prehistoric migration of the Celts from Asia, across North Africa, through Spain and France, to its conclusion in Scandinavia, their stone-culture endured along Atlantic's shores for some 2000 years before Gallic invaders fell upon them with their bronze swords. Then were deserted the aisle-like alignments, the cromlech's circle or semi-circle of menhirs, the house-like dolmen with slab-topped roof — three stone-forms probably having to do with orientation, worship, and sepulture — and the last of a primitive culture vanished into the realm of myths and latter-day superstition.

Still do Breton peasants place food on dolmens, lest their crops be blighted. Still do their old legends tell of the Korrigans, those Celtic dwarfs, who are supposed to revisit the dolmens they once inhabitated. And every child around Carnac has heard its stones called "the soldiers of St. Cornély," and knows the legend. That good saint, it appears, once travelled about in his ox-cart, bearing the blessing of God to the Celtic heathen; but near Carnac their soldiers chased him coastward until he was between the devil and the deep sea. Thereupon the saint arose in his cart and stretched forth a maledictory hand. "Ye stony deaf to God's word," he thundered, "be ye stones from henceforth!" And immediately the enfiled troops were transformed into those multiple parallel lines of cromlechs that stretch across Carnac's plain — or so say the legends of the Christian Fathers.

But why should the Church monopolize such delightful tales of miracles and retribution? The Celtic heathen must have had their legends, also. Indeed, it would not be hard to prove that, just as the early Church metamorphosed pagan heroes into Christian saints, so many a pious legend is but the anaemic offspring of some lusty, rousing tale, originally told by the Heathen Fathers.

How does hagiology so often start its fable? Thus: "Suddenly before the Breton peasant, as he knelt by the wayside Cross, appeared good St. Cornély." So, then, I have no hesitation in commencing a Heathen Father's fable by averring that, suddenly before the American tourist, as he sat inside one of Brittany's dolmens, appeared Stone-age Korrigan. Even as the peasant recognized St. Cornély by his crozier and halo, so the American tourist recognized Korrigan as a stone-age Celt by his buffalo-skin and stone-ax. Moreover, his flaming hair fell mane-like to his waist, and his eyes were blue and twinkly, and he spoke in that rich Celtic accent which the Irish, descendants of the Celts, use to this day.

"I'm Korrigan," he began, twirling his ax. "Why are yez threspassin' here, and will yez go quiet?"

"What!" exclaimed the American tourist. "Not *the* Corrigan family, building-contractors in the Bronx?"

"Not the same. We Korrigans have always been on the police-force here, keeping the O'Gallic thribes in order. I'm agin' the thribal form of governmint."

"Have a drink, officer!" said the American tourist, pulling a flask of Three-star Hennessy from his pocket.

"The Druidy priest says that anny officer looking on liquor while on duty will be strook blind," muttered Korrigan. "Nevertheless —." With that, he screwed his eyes tight shut, reached for the Hennessy, and took a manful swallow. "God knows I didn't look on it!" he breathed, handing back the flask.

"But weren't you Celts all turned by St. Cornély into Carnac's big stones?" asked the American tourist, consulting his guide-book.

"Divil a bit!" replied Korrigan, "'twas after us O'Celts came out of the East. A wandering race, we was, as the old prophecy went, fated to be the makings of lands we'd never own ourselves, and yet wit would save us at the last." Thoughtfully Officer Korrigan combed his flaming beard with a fishbone, then, after another swig at the flask, he related the following pious legend:

"Ye must know that the O'Celts was fairly rowlin' with riches until, passing through Agypt, they went to the ostrich-races and bet it all away. They then proceeded to these shores, but the O'Gallics mustered a big ar-rmy, so the undhrilled O'Celts remained on the beach, eating fish. Now, 'tis certain that fish only goes good with potatoes. Well, there was the O'Gallics' wide lands that 'ud be fine for potato-raising, except that they was covered, as thick as the hairs on your hand, with enor-rmous laying-down boulders.

"Well, 'twas me ancestor, high-priest Korrigan O'Korrigan, was the foxy lad. 'We're after thim big stones of yours,' says he to the O'Gallic chieftains, 'and we'll fight yez for them to the last man!' Now, that puzzled the simple O'Gallics. Me ancestor goes on, 'Haven't we come half way across the world for this priceless treasure? Beware lest the avaricious Britons get word of ut and despoil this Paradise of its last beautious rock!'

"Seeing that they possessed a priceless treasure unbeknownst to themselves, the O'Gallics began moving the rocks into the interior, which cleared the land for the O'Celts, and soon me forefathers was peacefully raising not only potatoes but all the illyments of their sacred thribal dish. 'Tis potatoes, and carr'ts, and beef-chunks, all stewed together, and may God forgive ye if ye lave out the onions!"

"Well, th' splendiferous smell av that thribal dish floated across to the inimy, an' they comes over and captures a potful. Ignorant of thruck-raisin' was the O'Gallics, and the eating of that stew was such that they begun diplomytizing for to annex the O'Celts potato-patches. 'Twas high-priest Korrigan O'Korrigan who averted hostilities. 'And you with a mighty power of rocks, over there, and don't know what to do with them!' says he, contemptuous-like. 'And what shud we do with them, thin?' asks the simple O'Gallics. 'Don't yez know,' says the holy man, 'that there's a magical spell must be done before growing potatoes? If ye had anny sinse, ye'd lay out them tens o' thousands o' great, magic stones in straight lines, fifty feet apart. But sure, I've no right to be telling ye, at all, at all!'

"So the thrustful O'Gallics returned and put their ar-rmy to stone-shifting. 'Twas a long job, and it gave the O'Celts five long years of peace and prosperity while dhrillin' an ar-rmy of their own. Thin the O'Gallics came over to fight us, saying the magic had been done but no potatoes was sprouting. And again me ancestor pacified thim. 'By the ass of Baalam,' says he, 'have ye laid thim stones *flat*? 'Tis standing up, they shud be, and it as different, speaking in magical terms, as milestones is from millstones!' says he.

"Praise God, it give the O'Gallics another year's wor-rk and the O'Celts another year of mil'try preparations! But at last 'twas done, and when me ancestor was summoned before the O'Gallics because no potatoes had sprouted, he tur-rns up with an army the like of which was never seen, so that the O'Gallics begun hiding behind the thousands of big, stood-up stones that was now in rows forming squares fifty paces to a side.

" 'Good!' says high-priest O'Korrigan, 'At last ye've cleared your soil for potato-raising, and the rest of the magic is that you'll pay us twinty percent av the crop, be way of gratichood. To each man of yez one of thim squares, making twinty thousand potato-patches in all. My blessings on yez!' says the holy man, lifting his hands in benediction. And he departed.

"And so was the ould prophecy fulfilled. We were the makings of a land we niver owned ourselves, and 'twas wit that saved us at the last."

Such is the Heathen Legend of Carnac. And in proof thereof (as the Christian legend of St. Cornély puts it) the stones remain there unto this very day.

Jan and Cora Gordon
The Dordogne: Food, Food 1943

AT Les Ézies also we had naturally to submit to the guide. In the case of the caves of Font-de-Gaume we were led by an old woman, who was clearly carrying out a routine duty and wanted to get back to her house as quickly as possible. But at Combarelles we found another type. The guide at Combarelles was a small, jocund hunchback, a leader singularly appropriate to the trolls' caverns he conducted us into, narrow clefts in the stone, through which at one time the explorers had to crawl on their stomachs. Already they have dug away the floor to give more head-room. And while we were there electricians, paid by a benefactor from distant Los Angeles, were installing electric light. We were among the last who would follow the troll, lighting ourselves with smoky dips stuck on to a piece of wood. But our troll had a family interest in the caves and drawings which made his guidance a thing of enthusiasms.

"My father used to own this cave," he said, "and many's the time I've crawled into it as a boy, little suspecting the treasures here. My father sold the cave to the Government for twenty pounds. Yes, twenty pounds, *m'sieur;* and they say the drawings are of inestimable value."

"He might have got a bit more than that for them," we said.

"*Eh, bien!*" answered the dwarf, with simple resignation. "It would be a question of having the cash to exploit them, you see. And if one hasn't that, what use are they?"

When we had reached the daylight once more, and we had given him a *pourboire,* he turned to his dog.

"Now," he said, "stand up and thank the lady and gentleman on my behalf."

The dog at once stood on its hind-legs and, wrinkling up its cheeks, gave us a most whimsical smile.

If, as the prehistorians affirm, these painted or carved beasts are really religious fetiches they were shaped for one purpose, that of charming the victims nearer to the spears, arrows, or death-falls of their devourers. Modern psychoanalysts hold, as a first element of faith, that the absorbing passion of humanity is sex. That is eminently a well-fed belief. Magdalenian man could have taught them that the first most urgent need is food, and that, suffering from a yammering tummy, no man goes out chasing the girls. Food, food. Even this splendidly carved horse in the hollow of Cap Blanc was no tribute to man's most efficient servant. The horse hadn't yet been promoted from the stew-pot, and the *boucherie chevaline* would not have been considered as low by the Stone Age cook, but a consummation devoutly to be hoped for.

Thus Magdalenian man comes into close contact with the most modern man, the man of the United States. Between that day and this few statues have been erected to animals as mere food-producers — except perhaps Romulus' and Remus' wolf. But the twentieth century A.D. joins hands with the two hundredth B.C. at Seattle, Washington, U.S.A. There a statue has been erected to "The Nourishing Mother of the Human Race," with the following inscription:

HERE LIVED AND SERVED HUMANITY
SEGIS PIETERTJE PROSPECT
Born 1913 . . . *Died* 1925
Twice she has registered records of production that have
raised her fame far above all that of other milking cows of
the age . . . Fathered by a king of the Holstein race, she
was herself the mother of sons and daughters of cham-
pion rank. Her royal value has deserved the gratitude in
the name of which this homage is offered . . .

The Stone Age man made his drawing in the hopes of smaller and less efficient woolly rhinoceroses, the Seattle man has erected his monument in the hopes of bigger and better udders; once more extremes meet. But the comment on Spanish modern popular art is equally applicable to Seattle. The cave man knew best.

And extremes meet again, for here where the Stone Age man first learned to singe the steaks of mammoth or of sabre-toothed tiger is now the land of Périgord, famous among gastronomers. Here you will find such dishes as hare stuffed with goose's liver, truffled turkey, soup of goose's carcass, *pâté* of partridges' livers, larded truffles cooked under the ashes, rusty sauce (of chicken's blood), rabbit with puffballs (but keep an eye on your toadstools), stuffed goose's neck, eels in verjuice, and many another dainty.

We tested none of them, for we were hastening upward and onward. . . .

Margaret Fishback
The Pyrenees: Midsummer
Melancholy *c1930*

Oh, somewhere there are people who
Have nothing in the world to do
But sit upon the Pyrenees
And use the very special breeze
Provided for the people who
Have nothing in the world to do
But sit upon the Pyrenees
And use the . . .

Charles Dickens
Avignon: Light in
the Oubliettes *1860*

HARD by the cathedral stands the ancient Palace of the Popes, of which one portion is now a common jail, and another a noisy barrack; while gloomy suites of state apartments, shut up and deserted, mock their own old state and glory, like the embalmed bodies of kings. But we neither went there to see state rooms nor soldiers' quarters, nor a common jail, though we dropped some money into a prisoners' box outside, whilst the prisoners themselves looked through the iron bars, high up, and watched us eagerly. We went to see the ruins of the dreadful rooms in which the Inquisition used to sit.

A little, old, swarthy woman, with a pair of flashing black eyes, — proof that the world hadn't conjured down the devil within her, though it had had between sixty and seventy years to do it in, — came out of the Barrack Cabaret, of which she was the keeper, with some large keys in her hands, and marshalled us the way that we should go. How she told us, on the way, that she was a Government officer (*concierge du palais apostolique*), and had been for I don't know how many years; and how she had shown these dungeons to princes; and how she was the best of dungeon demonstrators; and how she had resided in the palace from an infant, — had been born there, if I recollect right, — I needn't relate. But such a fierce, little, rapid, sparkling, energetic she devil I never beheld. She was alight and flaming, all the time. Her action was violent in the extreme. She never spoke, without stopping expressly for the purpose. She stamped her feet, clutched us by the arms, flung herself into attitudes, hammered against walls with her keys, for mere emphasis; now whispered as if the Inquisition were there still, now shrieked as if she were on the rack herself; and had a mysterious, hag-like way with her forefinger, when approaching the remains of some new horror — looking back and walking stealthily, and making horrible grimaces — that might alone have qualified her to walk up and down a sick man's counterpane, to the exclusion of all other figures, through a whole fever.

Passing through the courtyard, among groups of idle soldiers, we turned off by a gate, which this She Goblin unlocked for our admission, and locked again behind us, and entered a narrow court, rendered narrower by fallen stones and heaps of rubbish; part of it choking up the mouth of a ruined subterranean passage, that once communicated (or is said to have done so) with another castle on the opposite bank of the river. Close to this courtyard, is a dungeon — we stood within it, in another minute — in the dismal tower *des oubliettes,* where Rienzi was imprisoned, fastened by an iron chain to the very wall that stands there now, but shut out from the sky which now looks down into it. A few steps brought us to the Cachots, in which the prisoners of the Inquisition were confined for forty-eight hours after their capture, without food or drink, that their constancy might be shaken, even before they were confronted with their gloomy judges. The day has not got in there yet. They are still small cells, shut in by four unyielding, close, hard walls; still profoundly dark, still massively doored and fastened, as of old.

Goblin, looking back as I have described, went softly on, into a vaulted chamber, now used as a store-room, once the chapel of the Holy Office. The place where the tribunal sat, was plain. The platform might have been removed but yesterday. Conceive the parable of the Good Samaritan having been painted on the wall of one of these Inquisition chambers! But it was, and might be traced there yet.

High up in the jealous wall, are niches where the faltering replies of the accused were heard and noted down. Many of them had been brought out of the very cell we had just looked into, so awfully, — along the same stone passage. We had trodden in their very footsteps.

I am gazing round me, with the horror that the place inspires, when Goblin clutches me by the wrist, and lays, not her skinny finger, but the handle of a key, upon her lip. She invites me, with a jerk, to follow her. I do so. She leads me out into a room adjoining, — a rugged room, with a funnel-shaped, contracting roof, open at the top, to the bright day. I ask her what it is. She folds her arms, leers hideously, and stares. I ask again. She glances around, to see that all the little company are there; sits down upon a mound of stones; throws up her arms, and yells out, like a fiend, "La Salle de la Question!"

The Chamber of Torture! And the roof was made of that shape to stifle the victim's cries! O Goblin, Goblin, let us think of this awhile, in silence. Peace, Goblin! Sit with your short arms crossed on your short legs, upon that heap of stones, for only five minutes, and then flame out again.

Minutes! Seconds are not marked upon the Palace clock, when, with her eyes flashing fire, Goblin is up, in the middle of the chamber, describing, with her sunburnt arms, a wheel of heavy blows. Thus it ran round! cries Goblin. Mash, mash, mash! An endless routine of heavy hammers. Mash, mash, mash! upon the sufferer's limbs. See the stone trough! says Goblin. For the water torture! Gurgle, swill, bloat, burst, for the Redeemer's honour! Suck the bloody rag, deep down into your unbelieving body, Heretic, at every breath you draw! And when the executioner plucks it out, reeking with the smaller mysteries of God's own Image, know us for His chosen servants, true believers in the Sermon on the Mount, elect disciples of Him who never did a miracle but to heal; who never struck a man with palsy, blindness, deafness, dumbness, madness, any one affliction of mankind; and never stretched His blessed hand out, but to give relief and ease!

See! cries Goblin. There the furnace was. There they made the irons red-hot. Those holes supported the sharp stake, on which the tortured persons hung poised, dangling with their whole weight from the roof. "But," — and Goblin whispers this — "Monsieur has heard of this tower? Yes? Let Monsieur look down, then!"

A cold air, laden with an earthy smell, falls upon the face of Monsieur; for she has opened, while speaking, a trap-door in the wall. Monsieur looks in. Downward to the bottom, upward to the top, of a steep, dark, lofty tower, very dismal, very dark, very cold. The Executioner of the Inquisition, says Goblin, edging in her head to look down also, flung those who were past all further torturing, down here. "But look! does Monsieur see the black stains on the wall?" A glance, over his shoulder, at Goblin's keen eye, shows Monsieur — and would without the aid of the directing key — where they are. "What are they?" "Blood!"

In October, 1791, when the Revolution was at its height here, sixty persons, men and women ("and priests," says Goblin, — "priests"), were murdered, and hurled, the dying and the dead, into this dreadful pit, where a quantity of quick-lime was tumbled down upon their bodies. Those ghastly tokens of the massacre were soon no more; but while one stone of the strong building in which the deed was done remains upon another, there they will lie in the memories of men, as plain to see as the splashing of their blood upon the wall is now.

Was it a portion of the great scheme of Retribution that the cruel deed should be committed in this place! That a part of the atrocities and monstrous institutions which had been, for scores of years, at work to change men's nature should, in its last service, tempt them with the ready means of gratifying their furious and beastly rage! Should enable them to show themselves, in the height of their frenzy, no worse than a great, solemn, legal establishment, in the height of its power! No worse! Much better. They used the Tower of the Forgotten, in the name of Liberty, — their liberty; an earth-born creature, nursed in the black mud of the Bastille moats and dungeons, and necessarily betraying many evidences of its unwholesome bringing-up, — but the Inquisition used it in the name of Heaven.

Goblin's finger is lifted; and she steals out again, into the Chapel of the Holy Office. She stops at a certain part of the flooring. Her great effect is at hand. She waits for the rest. She darts at the brave Courier, who is explaining something; hits him a sound rap on the hat with the largest key; and bids him be silent. She assembles us all round a little trapdoor in the floor, as round a grave. "Voilà!" she darts down at the ring, and flings the door open with a crash, in her goblin energy, though it is no light weight. "Voilà les oubliettes! Voilà les oubliettes! Subterranean! Frightful! Black! Terrible! Deadly! Les oubliettes de l'Inquisition!"

My blood ran cold, as I looked from Goblin, down into the vaults, where these forgotten creatures, with recollections of the world outside, — of wives, friends, children, brothers, — starved to death, and made the stones ring with their unavailing groans. But the thrill I felt on seeing the accursed wall below, decayed and broken through, and the sun shining in through its gaping wounds, was like a sense of victory and triumph. I felt exalted with the proud delight of living, in these degenerate times, to see it. As if I were the hero of some high achievement! The light in the doleful vaults was typical of the light that has streamed in on all persecution in God's name, but which is not yet at its noon! It cannot look more lovely to a blind man newly restored to sight than to a traveller who sees it, calmly and majestically, treading down the darkness of that Infernal Well.

Tibor Koeves
Marseille: The Spice
of Europe 1939

MARSEILLE is the spice among the cities of Europe. You can't think, speak, write Marseille. You have to feel it, see it, above all smell it. Every city has its characteristic odors, from the lavender of Muenchen to the swampy dankness of Ravenna, perfumed Lausanne, oak-scented Bern, the rainy smell of Rouen, the sour atmosphere of Milan, and the rusty air of Hamburg. Yet nowhere are these smells so compelling, over-powering, and entrancing as in Marseille.

In Marseille your sense of smell dominates the scene. You'd think that all the amber, myrrh, incense, and resin brought here centuries ago by Greek settlers from the East had soaked into the earth, the way their scents assail you at every corner, mingled with the smell of oil, tar, tomatoes, fish, and brine. Take dinner in the open in the Vieux Port some evening, and your bouillabaisse will be as spicy as the waves breaking at your feet, as peppery as your host's remarks, as hot as the amazing vocabulary of urchins around you. For centuries natives hereabouts have imbibed the spices in their soil and air and filled their lungs, their hearts, their language with it. That airy intoxication that settled on the traveler there in the golden sunshine of a spring morning is the natural state of the city. Words, sighs, thoughts and laughter, joy and sorrow are spicy in Marseille.

Like pepper to the tongue, the inimitable 'assent' of Marseille will titillate your ear, the joyous look of teeming crowds on the Cannebière will rouse your eye, its humor and its joy of living will gladden your heart. Every taste and color is a shade more pronounced in Marseille. The dull grays of any other city are a silver pearly hue here, and the sky is a sparkling, brilliant blue. Everything is rhythm and music — not artistically perfect harmonies as in Naples, but something more human and personal if less polished.

The exotic aroma and pulses quickened by spice affect the most commonplace actions. You raise your hat feelingly, with a quick, triumphant flourish. Ordering a mug of beer becomes a romantic gesture; and the sight of a jungle film will give you the same thrill as a big-game hunting expedition in the wilds of Africa. Neighboring merchants, who for decades have been accustomed to open their shops at the exact same instant, greet each other every morning as if they had just returned from the Foreign Legion. If, perchance, any of them has seen a mouse the night before, the street pulses with drama as he tells the tale of his encounter with the dread monster; the five-ton lorry outside stands for his bed, his show window for a peep-hole, the big bronze doors of the church down the street for the door of his room, and a Saint Bernard led on a leash by his master becomes the mouse — that's how big the damned beast was. The audience listen with awe and wonder; they shake their heads, the story is after their own hearts. No one would think of doubting it; they only tell you that it 'takes Marseille.'

It takes a miracle of miracles to rate as a prodigy in Marseille. Therein is the wisdom of the city, and the surest guaranty of its happiness. In the absence of miracles, all things are marvels. The simplest actions — our speech, the way we draw breath, the heavenly flavors of vegetables, the pain of parting, and the joy of reunion — are all fraught with wonder. Day in and out the spirit of Marseille celebrates the miracle of blood coursing through our veins, the prodigy of seeing, hearing, touching, walking, feeling, sleeping and waking in an orgy of intoxication in the spicy air of the city.

S. J. Perelman
The Riviera: Life at
the Cafard 1950

LIFE at the Cafard was by and large uneventful; the seasonal tourist avalanche had not yet hit the Riviera, and outside a biweekly busload of Danish giantesses who smoked cheroots and ducked each other boisterously in the Mediterranean, the guests were mainly clandestine weekend couples and spidery young British actors in gay neckcloths. Everyone spent his waking hours on the strip of beach before the hotel, mangling his feet on the shifting pebbles or doggedly frying his midriff an angry scarlet in a vain effort to appear eupeptic. The French bathing suit, it was instructive to note, had been sheared down from my last memory of it to the irreducible minimum known as the Rasurel, a microscopic triangle laced across the hips and supplemented in the womenfold by an extremely sketchy bandeau. While undeniably hygienic, it was a costume demanding the flawless proportions of a Nita Naldi or Earle Lieder-man, and it was utterly merciless on anybody cursed with sheep-shanks or a prolapsed stomach, as were most of those who affected it. But excessive self-consciousness has never been a Latin frailty, and what might have aroused stupefaction elsewhere was here consid-ered merely *sportif*. This was especially the case with a young blood who appeared dramatically one day for an afternoon's spear-fishing, escorted by a sizeable retinue of attendants, masseurs, relatives, and well-wishers. He wore demi-Bikini shorts, rubber flippers on his hands and feet, a Cyclops underwater goggle with periscope attach-ment, and a wire like a zoot chain for receiving his catch. Brandish-ing the tubeful of poisoned arrows with which he manifestly planned to strike down his prey, he made a lengthy, declamatory speech of farewell, drank two Cinzanos, and having shaken hands all around, sailed gingerly into the water. The crowd watched tensely, shouting warnings and encouragement to the intrepid one as he plunged deeper. At about waist height, he turned, waved a final goodbye, and submerged. In all he remained below about four minutes, with three reappearances to draw breath. Then, puffing like a grampus (a grampus was puffing near by, so that I had some basis for compari-son), he staggered back to shore amid wild acclaim for his escape from a watery grave, announced that there were no fish to be had, embraced each member of the gallery in turn, drank another apéri-tif, and was triumphantly borne off to the café to relate his adven-tures, which, it was plain, bade fair to eclipse anything in Jules Verne.

Take one Nirvana with another, our choice of Beaulieu as a haven to careen in and chip the barnacles from our keels was fairly lucky. It was quiet, tidy, and above all, devoid of the Asbury Park *Schweine-rei*, the concentration of beachwear shops, pseudo-nautical bars, and frenetic casinos that had mushroomed at places like Saint Tro-pez, La Condamine, and Bandol. On our few forays into the latter, they all turned out to be full of intense young men in blue rope espa-drilles and surrealist chin-whiskers squabbling about Jean-Paul Sartre; where once the fishermen had spread their seines were now boogie-woogie and fried clams. Emotional Francophiles love to con-tend that it was American influence that cheapened the Riviera; to

my way of thinking, the fault lay with the French vacationists themselves, who no longer seemed capable of sipping a vermouth without
a radio blasting a light cavalry overture in the background and
whose sartorial lunacies surpassed anything at Palm Springs.
Beaulieu, as a matter of fact, was an ideal grandstand seat to observe
them at their most unhinged. From the sidewalk of the Bristol bar
any evening, you could watch them roar along the Lower Corniche
in explosive hot-rods piled with household effects, crash helmets
askew on their heads and lips skinned back with the diabolic appli-
cation of such boyhood heroes as Ralph di Palma or Teddy Tetzlaff.
They were on their way to Monaco to eat custard apples on a stick
and dance *le jitterbug,* and God help anyone who gainsaid them.

Harriet Beecher Stowe
The French Alps:
The Highest Dud in Europe 1854

I T is rather a discouraging reflection that one should travel three or
four hours to get to such a desolate place as these mountain tops
generally are; nothing but grass, rocks, and snow; a shanty, with a
show case full of minerals, articles of carved wood, and engravings
of the place for sale. In these show cases the Alps are brought to market as thoroughly as human ingenuity can do the thing. The chamois
figures largely; there are pouches made of chamois skin, walking
sticks and alpenstocks tipped with chamois horn; sometimes an
entire skin, horns and all, hanging disconsolately downward. Then
all manner of crystals, such as are found in the rocks, are served up
— agate pins, rings, seals, bracelets, cups, and snuffboxes — all
which are duly urged on your attention; so, instead of falling into a
rapture at the sight of Mont Blanc, the regular routine for a Yankee is
to begin a bargain for a walking stick or a snuffbox.

There is another curious fact, and that is, that every prospect loses
by being made definite. As long as we only see a thing by glimpses,
and imagine that there is a deal more that we do *not* see, the mind is
kept in a constant excitement and play; but come to a point where
you can fairly and squarely take in the whole, and there your mind
falls listless. It is the greatest proof to me of the infinite nature of our
minds, that we almost instantly undervalue what we have thoroughly attained. This sensation afflicted me, for I had been reining
in my enthusiasm for two days, as rather premature, and keeping
myself in reserve for this ultimate display. But now I stood there, no

longer seeing by glimpses, no longer catching rapturous intimations as I turned angles of rock, or glanced through windows of pine — here it was, all spread out before me like a map, not a cloud, not a shadow to soften the outline — there was Mont Blanc, a great alabaster pyramid, with a glacier running down each side of it; there was the Arve, and there was the Arveiron, names most magical in song, but now literal geographic realities.

But in full possession of the whole my mind gave out like a rocket that will not go off at the critical moment.

The Lyons Cathedral Clock

I should abstain from mentioning the curious clock in Lyons Cathedral, if it were not for a small mistake I made in connection with that piece of mechanism. The keeper of the church was very anxious it should be shown; partly for the honour of the establishment and the town, and partly, perhaps, because of his deriving a percentage from the additional consideration. However that may be, it was set in motion, and thereupon a host of little doors flew open, and innumerable little figures staggered out of them, and jerked themselves back again, with that special unsteadiness of purpose, and hitching in the gait, which usually attaches to figures that are moved by clock-work. Meanwhile, the Sacristan stood explaining these wonders, and pointing them out, severally, with a wand. There was a centre puppet of the Virgin Mary; and close to her, a small pigeon-hole, out of which another and a very ill-looking puppet made one of the most sudden plunges I ever saw accomplished; instantly flopping back again at sight of her and banging his little door violently after him. Taking this to be emblematic of the victory over Sin and Death, and not at all unwilling to show that I perfectly understood the subject, in anticipation of the showman, I rashly said, "Aha! The Evil Spirit, to be sure. He is very soon disposed of." "Pardon, Monsieur," said the Sacristan, with a polite motion of his hand towards the little door, as if introducing somebody, — "The Angel Gabriel!"
— *Charles Dickens, 1860*

"WE ALL RAISED A TREMENDOUS SHOUT."

❧Amusements

❧*Like the French themselves (there are one or two things we have in common with them, for example, the number of legs), we English-speaking folk go to the provinces not so much to sightsee as to amuse ourselves: to eat, gamble, mountain climb, and sunbathe. Think about it: if you're going to go through the nightmares that haunt trains, buses, and cars, you're gonna want something more than a church at the other end of the line. Most of all, you will want a great dinner, one of the ones you can never bring yourself to afford at home, but better. Though Paris is famous for its food and drink, it is from the provinces that it, and its chefs, come, and it is in the provinces that gourmets tour three-fork establishments.*

Alan Coren
Travelling Heavy 1983

JUST the other lunchtime, in a somewhat spatchcock biscuit-colored building on the narrow banks of the Veyle at Vonnas, a middle-aged man in a retina-wrinkling three-piece suit run up, at a guess, out of a bolt of old Black Watch curtaining, suddenly stood on his chair at the table next to mine and, after a full minute's fraught deliberation, photographed a prawn.

When he got down again, he turned to me, as if any explanation were necessary.

"Excuse me, sir," he said. His accent betokened the Great Plains; his voice was full of family bibles and wheat. "I hope I didn't disturb your lunch, it is just that I have always found it preferable not to go closer than four feet when photographing gourmet subjects."

I put down a tineload of *Pigeon de Bresse en Cocotte et Foie Blond Sauté*.

"I quite understand," I said. I have usually felt it prudent to choose civility as my best option when dealing with such people. They can be all smiles one minute, and stick an axe in your head the next.

"It is not," he said, clearly encouraged (always a risk), "that I do not carry a full range of auxiliary lenses, enabling me to get right down to within three inches, should the occasion demand it. I do." Here he indicated an anodised metal suitcase beside his chair, a compact monogrammed item not much larger than the average Portakabin. "It is simply that these introduce an unacceptable distortion factor."

"Yes," I said, "they would."

"Eat your pigeon," said my companion.

I have never known why they are always companions, in food articles. I have never known why food writers do not come right out and lay the relationship on the line. To me, a companion always sounds like someone you got out of a small ad in *The Lady* to hold your wool and make sure your bath-chair goes for its annual service. But there you are.

I moved the shard of bird-breast towards my lips.

"Are you by any chance a photographer, sir?" said the madman.

Why do elderly Americans call people sir? Are they after a tip? I put my fork down again.

"No," I said.

"My husband," said the madman's wife from across their table and through a display of flowers that, with her head in them, suggested something by Douanier Rousseau after a month or two on confiscated booze, "has photographed every three-star menu on our trip. We are from Gary, Indiana."

"I appreciate that," I said.

"I have three hundred gourmet slides already," said the husband. "I'll be giving an illustrated talk to the Elks when I get back."

He didn't say it with a capital E, of course; I realized it had one only later. At the time, it sounded no more unreasonable than anything else.

He sat down after that, but neither of them ate much. That wasn't really why they were there, in Georges Blanc's superb restaurant *La Mère Blanc,* a few miles north of Lyon. It is one of the problems of that handful of gourmet shrines for which Michelin trot out the three rosettes: more than mere great restaurants, they are now tourist cynosures, they are cultural artefacts to be seen, snapped, souvenired and taken back to Osaka and Surbiton on Kodak slide and commemorative ashtray. And just as Chartres Cathedral is packed to the gunwales with tourists who wonder why it comes to a point instead of having a rooftop burgerbar, just as the Mona Lisa is jostled by mobs wishing to know which shutter-speed Leonardo selected, so the great hallowed eateries of France now bear the burden of customers asking for bottles of ketchup and side-orders of sauerkraut.

They are, however, well-marshalled by the steely charm of the staff and thus obtrude hardly at all upon the preoccupations of the caring gutsies who have scuttled thither for the right reasons. And, if you like food at all, there is still no better place in all the world to be, when the mouse runs up the clock, than in one of the dozen-odd spots on whose owners' stove-tanned cheeks the men from the tyre company have plonked their acclamatory kiss. It is no mere design-coincidence that the Michelin symbol is a bloke with a big belly and a somewhat glazed smile.

Indeed . . . eating the best the French can bung at me has now become my only aim in travelling. I do not feel there to be a great deal of point in going anywhere else, or doing anything else when you get there. Much have I travell'd in the realms of gold, and many goodly states and kingdoms seen, the main legacy of which was the annual loss of the top level of skin and the bottom level of wallet, and few poignant memories to carry with me into life's reflective twilight. I have seen the Taj Mahal by moonlight and climbed the Great Pyramid of Giza, if that's the one on the right, I have crossed the Grand Canyon by mule, one of the most interesting acquaintances I met in Arizona, I have sweated in the Mato Grosso and cooled off in a Himalayan lake, admittedly not on the same day, I have stared at getting on for 13,000 paintings of the Madonna and Child. I have gone to the top of most things with steps, I have watched Indian television.

In thirty years, *en bref,* I have done my bit, and the remembered peaks that stick up above the fog of memory are a few French meals. Not my fault, we can't all be Patrick Leigh Fermor or Jan Morris, to take just three, what I like doing is tucking in, and henceforth I do not intend my holiday planning to go much further than M. Blanc's *Chaud-Froid de Foie Gras au Vin de Bordeaux, Bar de Ligne à la Marinière, Gratin de Homard Breton aux Huitres, Filet d'Agneau de Sisteron à la Crème de Champignons,* and *Marinade de Blanc de Poularde de Bresse Alexandre,* especially if I'm getting paid by the word . . .

Lyon. No city in the world is closer to more astonishing eating. On our second day, with the memory of Georges Blanc's unparalleled panwork still coming out of our pores like musk, we drove the fifty miles to Roanne and the legendary establishment of Les Frères Troisgros.

The eponymous Brothers Threefat, clearly marked from birth for a career in stuffing, have set up their stand opposite the railway station, with that occasionally irritating sans-souci with which the Frogs bang off the *grande geste*. Most of their best restaurants look from the outside like the kind of dumps a Berni patron wouldn't slow down for. It is possibly something to do with giving an impression of Art's priorities: remember what a sloppy dresser Van Gogh was?

I shall not dwell upon the astounding *bizarreries* that the Brothers managed to pull off that day. They do not, apart from anything else, translate well: mention Hot Gooseliver Salad and Sole Flutes, and the sensitive reader will reach for his enamel basin, but I should be failing in my duty to a paper of record if I did not put in a stunned word for their *Homard Poché à la fondue de Tomates et Concombres,* if only to reflect upon what an incredibly long way the lobster has come since man first stubbed his toe on that ludicrous piece of Meccano sidling along the sea-bed and decided, God knows how, that somewhere inside that pile of unprepossessing hinges there might be something worth eating.

Of the three restaurants visited, Threefat's was unquestionably (and engagingly) the least sacerdotal. It is essentially a local restaurant, full of bank managers with their sleeves rolled up and TVA inspectors with splashes of *sauce oursin* on their bi-focals; for the first time in my life, I heard a man at a neighbouring table, having watched his own companion mop up a third helping of duck, cry: "Tu es une bonne fourchette!" Is there anywhere else in the world that one adult publicly congratulates another on the sheer power of his eating?

That day, we stopped lunching at four. It seemed a good idea not to overdo it. Tomorrow, there was Bocuse, and you have to be in shape.

It is not easy culturally to translate Paul Bocuse. The chef as hero is a concept that does not travel: we should have to imagine a child produced by Ian Botham and the Queen Mother who grew up to take Port Stanley single-handed and win the Nobel Peace Prize for his television chat-show, and even then we should have but a poor British equivalent of the Renaissance colossus that is Paul Bocuse.

His court is in a lay-by ten kilòmetres from Lyon, in a dreary cleft between the railway and the Saône. It serves the best food in the world, and it is impossible for the sensitive soul not to be humbled in the presence of each arriving plate: this man, you say, is the greatest artist the oven has ever seen, his genius has produced this wondrous thing below my bib, and all I can do with it is stick it through a hole in my face. In an hour, I could be belching Rembrandt. *Eheu fugaces,* you murmur as the truffles wink, my name is Ozymandias, cook of cooks.

It slides down a treat, mind. Reverence is all well and good in its place, but after a moment or two saliva works its inexorable will and the cutlery flashes.

Soupe aux Truffes Noires, Loup en Croûte de la Mediterranée farci Mousse de Homard, Volaille de Bresse en Vessie, all come and go in the great orchestration of the gut's desire, tastes balanced and dovetailed, rhythms and reliefs counterpointed, and how are you going to break it to your tongue that it all ends tomorrow? Great cheeses melt down, *delices et gourmandises* in sweet pursuit, but he saves the best till last, he saves himself; what other *pièce de résistance* could top the meal but the mealmaker?

He shimmies from the wings, Toscanini not taking a bow so much as bestowing himself, a thick-muscled giant with an eagle's beak and a two-foot toque and the *Légion d'Honneur* around his throat, he has autographed your menu before you can stop him, he has pumped your hand, he can do ten languages, he is what the Pope could be if only he could cook, rapt Japs clap, he smiles and your spots clear up in seconds, you can play the piano again, he kisses your companion's trembling knuckle, he enquires whether you enjoyed your meal and if (his black eyes glitter) there is anything else you might conceivably want.

Like to try asking for the ketchup, Gary?

ꝫNot all French *cuisine is so* haute, *however; in fact, the most amusing and most well-remembered restaurants often are the regular, neighborhood, family-run bistros no one's ever heard of, where you are greeted not by a maître d' but by the family poodle (the full-size variety), the kind of place the delightful travel writer Ludwig Bemelmans rarely wrote about, except here.*

Ludwig Bemelmans
Les Saucissons d'Arles 1948

ꝫꝫ
O NE regrets," said the waitress of the restaurant Au Bon Coin in Arles, "but one has no saucisson d'Arles. There is a kind of saucisson d'Arles that I can offer Monsieur, but it is not the *vrai* saucisson d'Arles, which, as Monsieur undoubtedly knows, is made from the meat of donkeys."

The waitress, who had the face of the true Arlésienne — a narrow oval commanded by an aquiline nose that has a smaller upper and a longer lower concave edge — looked at me with the brown eyes that go with this type of face and waited for my answer. Since few things in this world are *vrai* any more and made of the stuff they once were, I ordered the imitation saucisson d'Arles.

"After the saucisson may I suggest, Monsieur, la truite au bleu," continued the waitress, handing me a soiled piece of cardboard with a kindergarten kind of writing on it. Then, pointing with her pencil stub, she said, "After the truite, perhaps the côtelette de veau Provençale with a small salad. As to the order for the dessert, I will come back for it. To drink I can recommend to Monsieur *le petit vin du pays*. It has no name, but it is a good, light wine."

She wrote out the order in the same hand in which the menu was written, on a block of cheap paper. I kept nodding and she turned after every dish and sang out its name in the direction of the kitchen. The cook was listening through a windowlike opening through which he had stuck his head, nodding acknowledgment of the orders from the other end.

Halfway between the table and the kitchen, behind a bar, sat a woman with the calm face of the Mona Lisa, who listened, smiling with approval, and after the wine was ordered she turned majestically to take a small carafe from a zinc-covered bar and filled this with the *petit vin du pays*.

The *Guide Michelin* lists no famous restaurants in this region, and I had come to the restaurant Au Bon Coin upon the recommendation of a taxi driver I found standing in front of the Hôtel Jules César, which is the best in Arles, comfortable, but not of the luxury class. The restaurant Au Bon Coin is located in an old building, to which a cement box has been added by way of a terrace. The terrace has four windows at each side and a set of French doors that run the width of the structure. There are no fly screens, and, as in all such establishments, the selection of the color or material of curtains has not troubled anyone much. The tables in such places are sometimes alike, but the chairs certainly vary in design, or else the chairs are the same and then the tables belong to several styles.

Here there were four small tables seating two people each, two tables for four, and one large enough to seat ten to twelve people. The parquet hardwood floor ended where the French doors folded back, and at that part it was much scraped and cut from the gravel which extended from the doors to the sidewalk. On the day of my visit two of the small tables were outside on the gravel, and the one at which I sat down was shaded by a nearby tree.

The chef, who looked like a young mechanic rather than a cook, accompanied the waitress, who carried the saucisson d'Arles, and he excused himself for allowing it to come out of his kitchen. "It is regrettable," he said, "that people who have come from such far-away places as America to eat the real saucisson d'Arles in its place of origin have to content themselves with an imitation," which, he explained, was made of pork. The waitress staggered back through the gravel, then walked on the hard floor and took a tray from a stack; the woman at the bar handed her the small carafe of wine, which was placed on the tray — together with a glass — and brought to the table.

Into one corner of the terrace leaned a man dressed like a groom; he wore a tattered sporting jacket several sizes too big and an old cap. He came to life as another man, dressed in the same fashion but in clothes that fitted, came running through the restaurant. The well-dressed one was busy pulling on gloves, and as he came out on the gravel he was met by a third man, who handed him a whip and led him to a waiting horse and cart. After a clicking sound and cracking his whip smartly, the man with the gloves sailed down the street behind his trotter. His jacket was visible long after the shape and the color of horse and wagon had become uncertain.

The sound of the hoofbeats fell away and the crunching of feet in the sands, to which I turned, announced the waitress, who poured the wine and asked for the bread ticket. I had just carefully detached the badly perforated token when the clop, clop, clop of the trotter was heard again, and as the horse came back up the boulevard, the entire staff of the restaurant ran to the door, the guests arose from their tables, and everybody shouted encouragement and praise. The cart went past, the driver lowered his whip in salute and smiled with ownership's pride. A puddle of water near the curb briefly mirrored his jacket.

"Monsieur is not eating his saucisson d'Arles?" said the waitress with concern as she turned to the table, after having waved at the horseman. She snapped her napkin at several dogs and eyed my table. "Go away, Diane. Give me peace, Azore," she shouted. As the dogs moved under the other tables and inside the restaurant the solicitous waitress said: "But they are not as bad as all that, the saucissons, monsieur." She pushed the plate toward me, put my fork on the plate atop the six thin slices of saucisson d'Arles, which resembled disks of greasy red marble, and then she went to another table, where she busied herself ladling potage santé into the plate of a man who had the unmistakable symptoms of a regular and satisfied patron of the establishment.

I poured myself another glass of wine from the cloudy glass jug, whose neck was full of fingerprints, and ate the sausages, which were good enough. Again the hoofbeats became audible, the staff once more rushed to the door, and this time the cart halted in front of the restaurant.

The magenta-colored nostrils of the horse distended and contracted; it was unhitched and taken to one of the trees, to which it was tied facing away from me, in a position that allowed it to swish the flies from its haunches as well as from my table.

The waitress came and wiped her face with the napkin and then threw it under her arm as she took away the plate on which the saucisson d'Arles had been. She said, "Don't derange yourself," forgetting the third-person address, "I shall be with you in a second and then I will not budge from this table again — the trout is on its way."

From then on, until the salad was cleared away, there was a crowd in front of and around my table, feeling the horse's legs and patting its rump. The chef found time to bring out carrot greens and feed them to the horse, and the owner stood with folded arms looking out into the street. Now and then he was almost pushed off the curb by the animal, which rubbed its head against the back of his multicolored tweed jacket.

He turned suddenly and put an end to the adoration of his horse by screaming for the waitress, whom he ordered to serve champagne to everyone. He took off the jacket and hung it over the vacant chair at my table and explained to me that he had acquired the horse that morning.

The Arlésienne let everything lie where it was and occupied herself with the order of the sportsman. She came back with champagne of an unknown brand, but, in the way of wine in France, nothing that comes out of a bottle is altogether bad, and this champagne, which had the color of thin light beer and its fragile white foam, was drinkable, and with the loud textiles it aided in establishing the free air of risk and reward that properly belongs around horses.

There was some singing later, and then after his coffee, whose piece of gray sugar he took from the saucer and sacrificed to his horse, the owner picked up his coat and, after brushing it with his hand, hung it over one shoulder. He untied the animal, looked at it once more, and led it away.

The waitress leaned against the tree and examined a bite on her arm inflicted by a horsefly.

"Who was that man?" I asked. She looked after him. He and the horse were stiffly walking down the exact center of the Boulevard des Lices.

"Oh, he," she said. "That is Monsieur the proprietor of this restaurant." She sucked the bite on her arm.

"And Madame," I asked, "is she the lady at the buffet?"

"*Non,*" answered the Arlésienne, "Madame and Monsieur have been divorced a long time. Madame lives in Paris."

I offer this overdetailed report on the character and personnel of this restaurant partly as a description of an average place in which I had a fair and reasonable meal, but chiefly to undo a cast-iron set of characters that live in the literature of travel. They are the half-witted, jovial owners of small restaurants and regional eating places who are usually called Papa or Mama, or *le bon Père So-and-so* or *la bonne Mère Catharine* or just *Monsieur le proprietaire* or *Madame la patronne.* They all suffer from the saccharine idiocy that infests Walt Disney's bunnies. Whether in Normandy, the Midi, or Provence, the cute innkeeper of these reports always comes out of his kitchen rubbing his hands to explain the *spécialités de la maison,* and Madame then comes trotting from behind her buffet, from her arrangements of homemade, delicious pâtés, her special céleri ravigotte, from the secrets of her small andouilles, her priceless tartelettes and macédoines. She joins *le bon père* at the table of the tourist, and with many sad "Ohs" and shakings of the head they both bleat about the bad times one lives in and add to this a recital of their occupational ills. Later they speak of the past, nodding now with nostalgia but saying "Ah," instead of "Oh." The conversation of these figures is as static as their design, and you will hear them speak as they do now in articles written in 1898. Now as then in these stories they agree with every opinion — religious, political, economic, scientific or gastronomic — which the guest puts forward, and as that one tears himself away to say adieu — always after the most memorable meal of his life — they both come to the tavern gate and wave after him. I have met all kinds of *hôteliers.* In my travels I have looked in vain for Monsieur and Madame.

P.S. Arles is a good city to come back to. The Saucissons d'Arles are real again.

≈Next to voyeurism, the most popular Riviera sin is gambling, not the glitzy, tourbus dissipation of Las Vegas and Atlantic City, but the extravagant, aristocratic prodigality of the principality of Monte Carlo, Monaco, just across a fantasy border that admits one to the age of chivalry and melodrama. Will Rogers and Alexander Woollcott — the prototypical Oklahoman and New Yorker, respectively — tell you everything you need to know to beat (or to join) the system.

Will Rogers
A Fish-Eye View of
Monte Carlo 1926

WELL, I had heard all my life of this pleasant and accommodating little place called Monte Carlo. We have heard all our life about "the Man that Broke the Bank at Monte Carlo." Well, I am down in Italy and I get caught in a tourist drive drifting north, and am swept right along with them. No man in the world is strong enough to buck a Tourist tide when it gets in full swing. They had visited all the old Churches in Mussoliniland, and they were looking for new Churches to conquer. They were just a-rarin' to see some more old ruins. "Bring on your ruins!" is the American Tourists slogan.

While they was headed for some old Cathedrals that they were "keeping standing for American trade," why I branches off over towards this Monte Carlo layout. I headed for a place called Nice. You know it's a kinder snorty place. All of them go to it in the winter time. Well, I get there and they give me a Hotel to myself. I was the sole support of it for days. So I commenced inquiring about Monte. Not that I was rarin' to speculate, but I wanted to see it so I could warn my readers just what numbers to play when you get there.

Well, this Monte Carlo is a queer layout. It's not only a Game, but it's a country. It's the only Country in the world that has practically no rural population. You either live in the City of Monte Carlo, or you don't live in Monaco. If you are out of town you are in France or Italy, or if you get too far out in the country you are in Spain or Switzerland. There is some pretty good ideas about the place. For instance, you don't have any taxes to pay. The Casino takes care of everything. When they told me that I said, "Why, how can they afford to do that?" The party I said that to laughed. I didn't know what he was laughing at then. I do now. They are not going short any, taking care of the principality of Monaco. They also won't let a fellow from the old home town go in and wager. He has to go to France to wager his excess tax money. Now that right there struck me as being a very fine trait in the government of Monaco.

They practically say to their own flesh and blood, "Stand back till we trim these suckers. If we need any extra for Yachts or Palaces we will let you home folks know, but we don't want to call on you till we absolutely have to." As to the business administration of the Casino, and its Senate and House of Representatives, they have never yet in all its history had to take a cent from home missions. Andy Mellon himself couldn't administer a financial program that would offer a larger balance at the end of six months.

I thought maybe it was going to be hard to get in there, but there is only one requirement and that is not so hard for an American to live up to. That is to answer, "Do you live in Monaco?"

I didn't think there was room for anyone else to live there unless they went out and annexed some more territory. You show your passport. Well, you do that anywhere over in Europe. Also if you have never written an Autobiography of your life, you haven't signed a foreign hotel register. All an American newspaper will have to do when you pass out and leave no record of yourself, they can get a continental register and add the date of death and it will give everything you ever did, and the great part of it is that it was written by yourself. Oh yes, at Monte they also collect a fee on entrance. If I lived a thousand years I will never know why they do that. It seems so unnecessary. Unless that entrance money goes to a different corporation. It is a very large building; that is, it's large for such a small country. They been wanting to put another wing on it, but France won't lease them the ground. As you go in you will see a beautiful big yacht floating majestically at the dock. It does not, as you might think belong to someone' who is playing there. It belongs to the Prince of Monaco. His Uncle ahead of him, who succeeded, died a year or so ago in what you wouldn't hardly call destitute circumstances, and this young man moved into the Palace and the family yacht. Due to the good feeling of all world the old fortune has not been allowed to dwindle away to any great extent.

His Uncle was a great fisherman, that was always touring over the world searching for strange fish. He has an Acquarium there showing them. Most of them are dead and stuffed. He didn't seem to be able to capture any alive, like he does there in the Casino. While he was away it never made much difference, as the business went on just the same. It's so well organized that it don't even need Edsel there to run it. They could cable him the receipts every morning.

There is only about three games to select from. I wanted to shoot a little Craps and take a hand at Stud Poker, but they just had a lot of women's games like Baccarat and Roulette. The Roulette wheel only had one 0 on it. That's what fooled me to the idea that it was pretty near on the level. Well, to make a fair bankroll short, it don't take me long to tell you I learned about the game pretty quick. If you ever in your life saw queer people they couldn't touch the ones there. Some of them they say had been there for years. Mostly old women. They would sit by the hour keeping track of what number come up and marking it down. They might not make one bet an hour. They seemed to have it timed perfectly, just when to lose. And I thought that was what they were doing, betting that they would lose, and a fellow said no they were playing a system, and they only bet at certain times. Well, they lose and then had some outside bet with someone that they would.

When I bet without a system, why they looked at me like I was crazy. I don't know why, because I was losing just as good as they were. There is one or two special rooms where the Americans or the bigger betters go. You pay extra to go in there. I tried it too. It was better than these common rooms. You could lose faster.

They have the prettiest chips you play with. I wanted some to bring home, so late at night when I was starting home, I cashed another Money Order and went over and bought 30 dollars worth of all denominations, and walked right by the tables rattling them and walked right on out. I showed 'em here was a Guy who wouldn't even go to the trouble of cashing in. I have their Chips. I haven't found out yet who the joke is on. They have a cliff there if you care for that particular branch of self-extermination. In fact, they have rigged up a Springboard so if you are going off you can get in an extra somersault on the way down. As I come out the old Yacht was waiting for Americans to Oil her up. The old prince has got a great business. It works while he sleeps.

Alexander Woollcott
Rien Ne Va Plus 1934

WE were sitting under the midsummer stars at Monte Carlo, eating a soufflé and talking about suicide, when a passing newsmonger stopped at our table all aglow with the tidings that the young American with the white forelock had just been found crumpled on the beach, a bullet-hole in his heart. Earlier in the evening — it was shortly before we came out of the Casino in quest of dinner — we had all seen him wiped out by a final disastrous turn of the wheel. And now he lay dead on the shore.

I shall have to admit that the news gave a fillip to the occasion. It came towards the end of a long, luscious dinner on the terrace opposite the Casino. We were a casually assembled carful, who had driven over from Antibes in the late afternoon, planning to play a little roulette as an appetizer and then to dine interminably.

When we had arrived in *Salles Privées* a few hours before, there was only standing room around our table at first. In this rapt fringe, I encountered Sam Fletcher, a dawdling journalist who lived on occasional assignment from the Paris offices of American newspapers. He pointed out the notables to me. There was Mary Garden, for instance, playing intently, losing and winning, losing and winning, with the economy of emotional expenditure which one usually reserves for setting-up exercises. Then there was an English dowager who looked as though she were held together by adhesive tape. She was betting parsimoniously, but Fletcher whispered to me that she lived in Monte Carlo on an ample allowance provided by her son-in-law, with the sole stipulation that she never embarrass the family by coming home. A moribund remittance woman. Next to her sat a pallid old gentleman whose hands, as they caressed his stack of counters, were conspicuously encased in braided gloves of gray silk. It seems that in his youth, he had been a wastrel, and, on her deathbed, his mother had squeezed from him a solemn promise never to touch card or chip again as long as he lived.

As for young White Lock, there was, until his final bet, nothing else noticeable about him except that he was the only man then at the table wearing a dinner coat. We heard later that at first he had lost heavily and had had to make several trips to the *caisse* to replenish his supply of plaques. By the time I came along he had settled to a more cautious play but finally, as if from boredom, he took all his plaques and counters and stacked them on the red. To this pile he added, just as the wheel began to turn, the contents of his wallet — emptying out a small cascade of thousand-franc notes, with a single hundred-franc note among them. But this one he retrieved at the last moment as if to be sure of carfare home. There was the breathless spinning moment, then the fateful *"Rien ne va plus,"* issuing in the same dead voice with which the intoning of the mass falls on infidel ears. Then the decision. *"Noir."* Around that table you could hear the word for black being *exhaled* in every language the world has known since Babel.

The young man gave a little laugh as the *croupier* called the turn. He sat quite still as his last gauge was raked into the bank. With all eyes on him, he shoved his chair back from the table, reached for his wallet, took out the aforesaid hundred-franc note and pushed it, with white, fastidious fingers, toward the center of the patterned baize. *"Pour le personnel,"* he said, with a kind of wry grandeur which hushed the usual twitter of thanks from the *croupiers*. "And that," he added, "is that." So saying, he got to his feet, yawned a little, and sauntered out of the room. I remember thinking, at the time, that he was behaving rather like any desperate young man in any Zoë Akins play. But it was a good performance. And now, it seems, he lay dead by the water's edge.

It was Fletcher himself who brought the news. It came, I say, just as we were eating soufflé and talking of suicide. This, of course, was no obliging coincidence. One always tells tall tales of self-slaughter at Monte Carlo. It is part of the legend of the principality — as strong in its force of suggestion, I suppose, as the legend of Lourdes is strong in its hint to hysterics that the time has come to cast away their crutches. Fletcher told us that the sound of the shot had brought a watchman running. The youth lay on his back, his chin tilted to the stars, one outstretched hand limply holding the revolver, a dark stain on the pleated whiteness of his breast. Before Fletcher could wire his report to Paris, he would have to await certain — well — formalities. In a conspiratorial whisper, he explained there had been so many such suicides of late that a new rule was but recently put into effect. Whenever any client of the Casino was found self-slain with empty pockets, it was customary for the Casino to rush a bankroll to the spot before notifying the police, so that the victim would seem to have ended it all from *Weltschmerz*. Even now, Fletcher said, this trick must be in progress, and in the meantime he ought to be seeking such obituary data as might be gleaned in the registry office.

We were still lingering over our coffee when he came hurrying back to us, all bristling with the end of the story. Notified in due course, the *gendarmerie* had repaired to the beach in quest of the body. But there was none. Not at the indicated spot, nor anywhere else on the shore. After further search, the minor chieftain from the Casino, who had himself tucked ten thousand francs into the pocket of the now missing suicide and was still lurking, much puzzled, in the middle-distance, returned at last to the *Salles Privées,* only to find them humming with a new chapter. It seems that young American with the white forelock — the one somebody or other had inaccurately reported as killed — had reappeared apparently restored in spirits, and certainly restored in funds. He had bet tremendously, lingered for only three turns of the wheel, and departed with a hundred thousand francs. The attendants assumed he had merely been out to dinner. At least the careless fellow had spilled some tomato sauce on his shirt-front.

There may not be a lot of them, many of them may be shared with Italy, but the French made sure they were at least the highest in Europe. I am referring, of course, to the French Alps and, in particular, to the biggest cheese of them all, Mont Blanc. To miss Mont Blanc is like missing Niagara Falls, Big Ben, or the Dead Sea. To simply look up at a mountain that high is like driving by the Dead Sea: you've got to get out and go for a swim or, in this case, go to the top. There are three ways to climb Mont Blanc. In descending (or, should I say, ascending) order of difficulty, they are: by foot (foolhardy), by téléphérique, or cable-car (only funny if the cable breaks), and by . . . well, only Mark Twain could have thought of it.

Mark Twain
Climbing Mont Blanc 1880

AFTER breakfast, that next morning in Chamonix, we went out in the yard and watched the gangs of excursionizing tourists arriving and departing with their mules and guides and porters; then we took a look through the telescope at the snowy hump of Mont Blanc. It was brilliant with sunshine, and the vast smooth bulge seemed hardly five hundred yards away. With the naked eye we could dimly make out the house at the Pierre Pointue, which is located by the side of the great glacier, and is more than 3,000 feet above the level of the valley; but with the telescope we could see all its details. While I looked, a woman rode by the house on a mule, and I saw her with sharp distinctness; I could have described her dress. I saw her nod to the people of the house, and rein up her mule, and put her hand up to shield her eyes from the sun. I was not used to telescopes; in fact I never had looked through a good one before; it seemed incredible to me that this woman would be so far away. I was satisfied that I could see all these details with my naked eye; but when I tried it, that mule and those vivid people had wholly vanished, and the house itself was become small and vague. I tried the telescope again, and again everything was vivid. The strong black shadows of the mule and the woman were flung against the side of the house, and I saw the mule's silhouette wave its ears.

The telescopulist, — or the telescopulariat, — I do not know which is right, — said a party were making the grand ascent, and would come in sight on the remote upper heights, presently; so we waited to observe this performance.

Presently I had a superb idea. I wanted to stand with a party on the summit of Mont Blanc, merely to be able to say I had done it, and I believed the telescope could set me within seven feet of the uppermost man. The telescoper assured me that it could. I then asked him how much I owed him for as far as I had got? He said, one franc. I asked him how much it would cost me to make the entire ascent? Three francs. I at once determined to make the entire ascent. But first I inquired if there was any danger? He said no, — not by telescope; said he had taken a great many parties to the sumit, and never lost a man. I asked what he would charge to let my agent go with me, together with such guides and porters as might be necessary? He said he could let Harris go for two francs; and that unless we were unusually timid, he should consider guides and porters unnecessary; it was not customary to take them, when going by telescope, for they were rather an incumbrance than a help. He said that the party now on the mountain were approaching the most difficult part, and if we hurried we should overtake them within ten minutes, and could then join them and have the benefit of their guides and porters without their knowledge, and without expense to us.

I then said we could start immediately. I believe I said it calmly, though I was conscious of a shudder and of a paling cheek, in view of the nature of the exploit I was so unreflectingly engaging in. But the old dare-devil spirit was upon me, and I said that as I had committed myself I would not back down; I would ascend Mont Blanc if it cost me my life. I told the man to slant his machine in the proper direction and let us be off.

Harris was afraid and did not want to go, but I heartened him up and said I would hold his hand all the way; so he gave his consent, though he trembled a little at first. I took a last pathetic look upon the pleasant summer scene about me, then boldly put my eye to the glass and prepared to mount among the grim glaciers and the everlasting snows.

We took our way carefully and cautiously across the great Glacier des Bossons, over yawning and terrific crevasses and amongst imposing crags and buttresses of ice which were fringed with icicles of gigantic proportions. The desert of ice that stretched far and wide about us was wild and desolate beyond description, and the perils which desert us were so great that at times I was minded to turn back. But I pulled my pluck together and pushed on.

We passed the glacier safely and began to mount the steeps beyond, with great celerity. When we were seven minutes out from the starting point, we reached an altitude where the scene took a new aspect; an apparently limitless continent of gleaming snow was tilted heavenward before our faces. As my eye followed that awful acclivity far away up into the remote skies, it seemed to me that all I had ever seen before of sublimity and magnitude was small and insignificant compared to this.

We rested a moment, and then began to mount with speed. Within three minutes we caught sight of the party ahead of us, and stopped to observe them. They were toiling up a long, slanting ridge of snow — twelve persons, roped together some fifteen feet apart, marching in single file, and strongly marked against the clear blue sky. One was a woman. We could see them lift their feet and put them down; we saw them swing their alpenstocks forward in unison, like so many pendulums, and then bear their weight upon them; we saw the lady wave her handkerchief. They dragged themselves upward in a worn and weary way, for they had been climbing steadily from the Grand Mulets, on the Glacier des Bossons, since three in the morning, and it was eleven, now. We saw them sink down in the snow and rest, and drink something from a bottle. After a while they moved on, and as they approached the final short dash of the home-stretch we closed up on them and joined them.

Presently we all stood together on the summit! What a view was spread out below! Away off under the northwestern horizon rolled the silent billows of the Farnese Oberland, their snowy crests glinting softly in the subdued lights of distance; in the north rose the giant form of the Wobblehorn, draped from peak to shoulder in sable thunderclouds; beyond him, to the right, stretched the grand processional summits of the Cisalpine Cordillera, drowned in a sensuous haze; to the east loomed the colossal masses of the Yodelhorn, the Fuddlehorn and the Dinnerhorn, their cloudless summits flashing white and cold in the sun; beyond them shimmered the faint far line of the Ghauts of Jubbelpore and the Aiguilles des Alleghenies; in the south towered the smoking peak of Popocatapetl and the unapproachable altitudes of the peerless Scrabblehorn; in the west-southwest the stately range of the Himmalayas lay dreaming in a purple gloom; and thence all around the curving horizon the eye roved over a troubled sea of sunkissed Alps, and noted, here and there, the noble proportions and soaring domes of the Bottlehorn, and the Saddlehorn, and the Shovelhorn, and the Powderhorn, all bathed in the glory of noon and mottled with softly-gliding blots, the shadows flung from drifting clouds.

Overcome by the scene, we all raised a triumphant, tremendous shout, in unison. A startled man at my elbow said, —

"Confound you, what do you yell like that, for, right here in the street?"

That brought me down to Chamonix, like a flirt. I gave that man some spiritual advice and disposed of him, and then paid the telescope man his full fee, and said that we were charmed with the trip and would remain down, and not re-ascend and require him to fetch us down by telescope. This pleased him very much, for of course we could have stepped back to the summit and put him to the trouble of bringing us home if we had wanted to.

I judged we could get diplomas, now, anyhow; so we went after them, but the Chief Guide put us off, with one pretext or another, during all the time we staid in Chamonix, and we ended by never getting them at all. So much for his prejudice against people's nationality. However, we worried him enough to make him remember us and our ascent for some time. He even said, once, that he wished there was a lunatic asylum in Chamonix. This shows that he really had fears that we were going to drive him mad. It was what we intended to do, but lack of time defeated it.

I cannot venture to advise the reader one way or the other, as to ascending Mont Blanc. I say only this: if he is at all timid, the enjoyments of the trip will hardly make up for the hardships and sufferings he will have to endure. But if he has good nerve, youth, health, and a bold firm will, and could leave his family comfortably provided for in case the worst happened, he would find the ascent a wonderful experience, and the view from the top a vision to dream about, and tell about, and recall with exultation all the days of his life.

While I do not advise such a person to attempt the ascent, I do not advise him against it. But if he elects to attempt it, let him be warily careful of two things: choose a calm clear day; and do not pay the telescope man in advance. There are dark stories of his getting advance-payers on the summit and then leaving them there to rot.

Love At The Beach

*B*athing here is carried on in quite a sociable manner: you may see parties of a dozen in the water, making a complete briny fête of it. Throwing cold water upon love, in our country, is supposed to have quite a chilling effect on the flame, if not to act as its entire extinguisher; here, it is quite au contraire: a gentleman dives with a lady, and "proposes" underwater (that they should *come up again,* I fancy, if his submarine eloquence extends so far). The flirtations I saw en caleçons were numerous, and I have no doubt pathetic; if the *sobbing* I heard at times was any criterion of the patient's case, I should think it was next to hopeless. The depth of the affaires du coeur that came before my notice varied from three to thirty feet, and though all flattered themselves they took things coolly, I saw many of both sufferers who were decidedly "over head and ears." — *Sylvanus (Robert Colton), 1846*

CIVIL SERVICE!

ꝑroblems

Any guidebook can warn the prospective tourist of the problems he might encounter on his vacation, but only a humorful one can truly prepare him for the inevitable. Take the French bureaucracy. Please. You will encounter it, much as Emily Kimbrough, James Thurber, and Laurence Sterne do in the following tales. It is up to you to decide whether your encounters will keep you awake at night with anger and frustration or provide you with stories to tell back home (of course, humorists, famous for the spontaneous overflow of their powerful feelings recollected in tranquillity — that's either Wordsworth or Groucho; no, Groucho never knew tranquillity — tend to do both; but you don't want to be a humorist, do you?).

Emily Kimbrough
The Post Office of
St. Florentin 1968

OTHER tourists who have visited St. Florentin remember the cathedral. It is starred in the guidebook. The post office is not mentioned, but it is the building Emily, Brother and I will remember and for all time associate with the town. We spent there a period of time whose minutes were not winged but fitted with the leaden shoes of a diver. Nevertheless, the visit was rewarding. When we came away, we had bought stamps . . .

The post office of St. Florentin stands on a corner where two streets converge sharply. It is not much to look at from the outside and has a dismal interior. My relatives joined a line standing in front of a grilled window with the sign "Timbres" above it. I sat down on a bench against the wall. Had I not done that because my legs were tired I might have missed two signs that gave me deep pleasure. One identified the section below it as the "Caisse Nationale de Prévoyance." By my translation this is the National Counter or Cash Room of Foresight. If I were French, I thought, I would find it reassuring to know there was a place in my local post office to which I could go when I needed foresight on a national scale. On another wall I read a framed illustrated announcement of a telegraph service. "These Illustrated Telegrams Deluxe," it read, "carry a surtax of the heart." The reproduction of this illustrated telegram deluxe included in one corner a large bouquet of flowers in staggeringly bright and assorted colors. Have we in America, I asked myself, a surtax on the heart carried by telegram? And I answered myself no. While I was ruminating enviously on the benefits France was offering, Brother and Emily reached the head of the line and almost immediately summoned me. Emily's eyes, very brown and very large, were more than ever like a startled deer's.

"I think the man is telling us," she said when I had reached them, "I cannot send these letters and postcards airmail to America."

She indicated the pile of mail she had pushed under the window to a thin elderly clerk whose eyes were not so large but as apprehensive as Emily's.

Brother was nodding agreement. "That's what I think he's saying."

I addressed myself in French to the clerk. "Is it possible, monsieur," I inquired, "that it is not possible to send these letters and postcards to the United States by airmail?"

The old gentleman spread tremulous hands palm upward and lifted his shoulders to his ears.

"Ah, madame," he said, "it is not certainly that it is not possible, it is only that I have not the proper stamps. It is therefore necessary that I make the computations among stamps of other prices to arrive at the proper number and amount, is it not?"

Certainly it was. I let him know I was with him.

"Then, madame," he continued, extending a hand toward me to make us one in understanding, "certainly you will know that this will have need of time and of work and it might be that you are pressed," the soft brown eyes were pleading pitifully, "and do not have the time for waiting and so you would take the ordinary stamps that I have do you see at my hand and if the messages are perhaps not so important?" His voice trailed up to a hopeful question.

Three heads shaken in unison convinced him there was no way out. Nevertheless, I explained. It is a failing of which I am often accused.

"You see, monsieur," I told him, "we come from the United States very far away. I have twin daughters; each is married, I have seven grandchildren. This is my brother and sister-in-law," indicating my companions. "They too have children, a son and a daughter. The son is married and they are expecting their first baby."

"Why don't you tell him you were born in Muncie, Indiana," Brother muttered," and that I went to Yale?"

I ignored the interruption.

"So you see we do not write these letters to amuse ourselves. They are to say we are well and that everything marches, so the young mother expecting her baby can remain tranquil and that my grandchildren can have education from the postcards of the beautiful places in your country we are seeing and so everything must go quickly."

The old man sighed deeply. "It is indeed so," he conceded and drew up a high stool.

From a drawer beneath the counter he took a copybook such as children use at school. He closed the drawer and seated himself on the stool, drawing it to the counter. Stretching as far as the bars of the window would permit because I wanted to watch this undertaking, I saw him twist his legs around the rungs of the stool, a substitute I thought for a clenched fist, that would emphasize his determined saying to himself, "If this thing has got to be done let's get on with it."

From arm's reach he brought a memorandum pad and placed it beside the copybook — meticulously because he shifted it three times. This pad was an assemblage of small pieces of paper, backs of envelopes, scraps of stationery, brown pieces, undoubtedly left over from wrapping a package. They were held together by a string run through a hole that had been punched in the top of each.

From a rack in front of him the mathematician selected three pencils, but the selections were not entirely to his liking. He took a penknife from the same tray, opened it carefully and certainly slowly, placed each pencil in turn point down on the top sheet of the memorandum pad and, bending low over it to gauge exactly how far to go, sharpened the point. He arranged the pencils in a row at the top of and just beyond the copybook, eased the pad to the edge of counter, blew delicately the graphite to the floor, waved the pad in the air, inspecting it between times, and only when it bore no trace of the recent operation performed on it, replaced it as meticulously as he had selected its position. Evidently there was no further delay that occurred to him. With a heartrending sigh he opened the copybook. It held between the pages the stamp supply, the denominations separated. I am sure the greatest number of these could not have been more than twenty. There was no index, even homemade, to show between what pages what stamps or any stamps could be found. So our lightning calculator had to turn each one in order to find and spread before him the material for his figuring.

The post office of St. Florentin will have to make a new memorandum pad. This one can never be used again. Both sides of every sheet were covered with figures; the pencils had to be resharpened.

Something, perhaps a telepathic cry for help, attracted the notice of the postmaster. Through an open door behind the counter I had seen a man with an air and position of authority, seated at a large flat desk. He rose, came without haste to the clerk, leaned forward, patted his shoulder, made an inquiry in a low tone. The clerk without looking up nodded miserably and showed the array of stamps spread before him and his calculations. The postmaster patted him again, returned to his inner sanctum and reappeared a minute later with a sheet of airmail stamps of the denominations proper for America. Evidently these were so precious he must have kept them put away in a safe.

Though pathetically grateful for his salvation, the clerk now had to start his calculations all over again, not, however, before he had returned to their proper places all the stamps he had accumulated — each denomination between two pages in the copybook. After this he dove again into figures. He was no wizard at addition but after three or four tries he reached a sum he liked or at least accepted and we did not question it.

Coming out of the building we were surprised to find it was still daylight. On our way to the barge we overtook Frances and Sophy, Frances triumphant because she had found a workman's blouse. Sophy, commissioned by Cornelia, had bought one for her. I was not happy to learn they had loitered at a number of antique shops and I did not care to hear what the others had done.

When we came on the barge Margalo and Romney were playing solitaire at separate tables; Emma was behind the bar. Nothing had changed. I wondered if this was the way it had seemed to Marco Polo returning.

As I started down the stairs to my cabin Emma called: "Richard wants me to tell everyone we now have a supply of stamps on board. You can buy them from me."

Laurence Sterne
Vexation upon Vexation 1759

To those who call vexations, VEXATIONS, as knowing what they are, there could not be a greater, than to be the best part of a day in *Lyons*, the most opulent and flourishing city in *France*, enriched with the most fragments of antiquity—and not be able to see it. To be withheld upon *any* account, must be a vexation; but to be withheld *by* a vexation——must certainly be, what philosophy justly calls

VEXATION

upon

VEXATION.

I had got my two dishes of milk coffee (which by the bye is excellently good for a consumption, but you must boil the milk and coffee together—otherwise 'tis only coffee and milk)—and as it was no more than eight in the morning, and the boat did not go off till noon, I had time to see enough of *Lyons* to tire the patience of all the friends I had in the world with it. I will take a walk to the cathedral, said I, looking at my list, and see the wonderful mechanism of this great clock of *Lippius* of *Basil*, in the first place——. . .

Taking a dozen or two of longer strides than usual across my room, just whilst it passed my brain, I walked down calmly into the *Basse Cour*, in order to sally forth; and having called for my bill—as it was uncertain whether I should return to my inn, I had paid it——had moreover given the maid ten sous, and was just receiving the dernier compliments of Monsieur *Le Blanc*, for a pleasant voyage down the *Rhône*——when I was stopped at the gate——

'Twas by a poor ass who had just turned in with a couple of large panniers upon his back, to collect eleemosunary turnip tops and cabbage leaves; and stood dubious, with his two forefeet on the inside of the threshold, and with his two hinder feet towards the street, as not knowing very well whether he was to go in, or no.

Now, 'tis an animal (be in what hurry I may) I cannot bear to strike——there is a patient endurance of sufferings, wrote so unaffectedly in his looks and carriage, which pleads so mightily for him, that it always disarms me; and to that degree, that I do not like to speak unkindly to him: on the contrary, meet him where I will— whether in town or country—in cart or under panniers—whether in liberty or bondage——I have ever something civil to say to him on my part; and as one word begets another (if he has as little to do as

I)——I generally fall into conversation with him; and surely never is my imagination so busy as in framing his responses from the etchings of his countenance—and where those carry me not deep enough——in flying from my own heart into his, and seeing what is natural for an ass to think—as well as a man, upon the occasion. In truth, it is the only creature of all the classes of beings below me, with whom I can do this: for parrots, jackdaws, *&c.*——I never exchange a word with them——nor with the apes, *&c.* for pretty near the same reason; they act by rote, as the others speak by it, and equally make me silent: nay my dog and my cat, though I value them both——(and for my dog he would speak if he could)—yet some how or other, they neither of them possess the talents for conversa-tion——I can make nothing of a discourse with them, beyond the *proposition*, the *reply*, and *rejoinder*, which terminated my father's and my mother's conversations, in his beds of justice——and those utter'd—there's an end of the dialogue——

—But with an ass, I can commune for ever.

Come *Honesty*! said I,—seeing it was impracticable to pass betwixt him and the gate——art thou for coming in, or going out?

The ass twisted his head round to look up the street—

Well—replied I—we'll wait a minute for thy driver:

——He turned his head thoughtful about, and looked wistfully the opposite way——

I understand thee perfectly; answered I——if thou takest a wrong step in this affair, he will cudgel thee to death——Well! a minute is but a minute, and if it saves a fellow creature a drubbing, it shall not be set down as ill-spent.

He was eating the stem of an artichoke as this discourse went on, and in the little peevish contentions of nature betwixt hunger and unsavouriness, had dropt it out of his mouth half a dozen times, and pick'd it up again——Go help thee, Jack! said I, thou hast a bitter breakfast on't—and many a bitter day's labour— and many a bitter blow, I fear, for its wages——'tis all—all bitterness to thee, whatever life is to others.——And now thy mouth, if one knew the truth of it, is as bitter, I dare say, as soot—(for he had cast aside the stem) and thou has not a friend perhaps in all this world, that will give thee a macaroon.——In saying this, I pull'd out a paper of 'em, which I had just purchased, and gave him one—and at this moment that I am telling it, my heart smites me, that there was more of pleasantry in the conceit, of seeing *how* an ass would eat a macaroon——than of benevolence in giving him one, which presided in the act.

When the ass had eaten his macaroon, I press'd him to come

in——the poor beast was heavy loaded——his legs seem'd to trem-
ble under him——he hung rather backwards and as I pull'd at his
halter, it broke short in my hand——he look'd up pensive in my face
——"Don't thrash me with it—but if you will, you may"——If I do,
said I, I'll be d——d.

The word was but one half of it pronounced, like the abbess of
Andoüillets—(so there was no sin in it)—when a person coming in,
let fall a thundering bastinado upon the poor devil's crupper, which
put an end to the ceremony.

Out upon it!

cried I——but the interjection was equivocal——and, I think wrong
placed too—for the end of an osier which had started out from the
contexture of the ass's pannier, had caught hold of my breeches
pocket as he rush'd by me, and rent it in the most disasterous direction you can imagine——so that the

Out upon it! in my opinion, should have come in here——but this
I leave to be settled by

The
REVIEWERS
of
MY BREECHES.

which I have brought over along with me for that purpose.

When all was set to rights, I came down stairs again into the *basse
cour* with my *valet de place,* in order to sally out towards the tomb of
the two lovers, *&c.*—and was a second time stopp'd at the
gate——not by the ass—but by the person who struck him; and
who, by that time, had taken possession (as is not uncommon after a
defeat) of the very spot of ground where the ass stood.

It was a commissary sent to me from the post-office, with a
rescript in his hand for the payment of some six livres odd sous.

Upon what account? said I.——'Tis upon the part of the king,
replied the commissary, heaving up both his shoulders——

——My good friend, quoth I——as sure as I am I—and you are
you——

——And who are you? said he.————Don't puzzle me; said I.

——But it is an indubitable verity, continued I, addressing myself
to the commissary, changing only the form of my asseveration
——that I owe the king of France nothing but my good-will; for he is
a very honest man, and I wish him all health and pastime in the
world——

Pardonnez moi—replied the commissary, you are indebted to him
six livres four sous, for the next post from hence to St. *Fons,* in your

rout to *Avignon*—which being a post royal, you pay double for the horses and position—otherwise 'twould have amounted to no more than three livres, two sous——

——But I don't go by land; said I.

——You may if you please; replied the commissary——

Your most obedient servant——said I, making him a low bow——

The commissary, with all the sincerity of grave good breeding—made me one, as low again.——I never was more disconcerted with a bow in my life.

——The devil take the serious character of these people! quoth I—(aside) they understand no more of IRONY that this——

The comparison was standing close by with his panniers—but something seal'd up my lips—I could not pronounce the name —

Sir, said I, collecting myself—it is not my intention to take post——

—But you may—said he, persisting in his first reply—you may take post if you chuse——

—And I may take salt to my pickled herring, said I, if I chuse——

—But I do not chuse —

—But you must pay for it, whether you do or no——

Aye! for the salt; said I (I know)——

—And for the post too; added he. Defend me; cried I——

I travel by water—I am going down the *Rhône* this very afternoon—my baggage is in the boat—and I have actually paid nine livres for my passage——

C'est tout egal—'tis all one; said he.

Bon Dieu! what, pay for the way I go! and for the way I do *not* go!

——*C'est tout egal;* replied the commissary——

——The devil it is! said I—but I will go to ten thousand *Bastiles* first——

O England! England! thou land of liberty and climate of good sense, thou tenderest of mothers—and gentlest of nurses, cried I, kneeling upon one knee, as I was beginning my apostrophe——

When the director of Madam *Le Blanc's* conscience coming in at that instant, and seeing a person in black, with a face as pale as ashes, at his devotions—looking still paler by the contrast and distress of his drapery—ask'd, if I stood in want of the aids of the church——

I go by WATER—said I—and here's another will be for making me pay for going by OYL.

As I perceived the commissary of the post-office would have his six livres four sous, I had nothing else for it, but to say some smart things upon the occasion, worth the money: And so I set off thus——

——And pray Mr. Commissary, by what law of courtesy is a defenceless stranger to be used just the reverse from what you use a *Frenchman* in this matter?

By no means; said he.

Excuse me; said I—for you have begun, sir, with first tearing off my breeches—and now you want my pocket——

Whereas—had you first taken my pocket, as you do with your own people—and then left me bare a —'d after—I had been a beast to have complain'd——

As it is——

——'Tis contrary to the law of *nature.*

——'Tis contrary to *reason.*

——'Tis contrary to the GOSPEL.

But not to this—said he—putting a printed paper into my hand.

PAR LE ROY.

—— ——'Tis a pithy prolegomenon, quoth I—and so read on —

— —
— —
— — — — — —

——By all which it appears, quoth I, having read it over, a little too rapidly, that if a man sets out in a post-chaise from *Paris*—he must to on travelling in one, all the days of his life—or pay for it.——Excuse me, said the commissary, the spirit of the ordinance is this—That if you set out with an intention of running post from *Paris* to *Avignon, &c.* you shall not change that intention or mode of travelling, without first satisfying the fermiers for two posts further than the place you repent at—and 'tis founded, continued he, upon this, that the REVENUES are not to fall short through your *fickleness*——

——O by heavens! cried I—if fickleness is taxable in *France*—we have nothing to do but make the best peace with you we can —

AND SO THE PEACE WAS MADE;

——And if it is a bad one—as *Tristram Shandy* laid the corner stone of it—nobody but *Tristram Shandy* ought to be hanged.

Though I was sensible I had said as many clever things to the commissary as came to six livres four sous, yet I was determined to note down the imposition amongst my remarks before I retir'd from the place; so putting my hand into my coat pocket for my remarks— (which by the bye, may be a caution to travellers to take a little more care of *their* remarks for the future) "my remarks were *stolen*"— Never did sorry traveller make such a pother and racket about his remarks as I did about mine, upon the occasion.

Heaven! earth! sea! fire! cried I, calling in every thing to my aid but what I should——My remarks are stolen!—what shall I do? Mr. Commissary! pray did I drop any remarks as I stood besides you!——

You dropp'd a good many very singular ones; replied he——Pugh! said I, those were but a few, not worth above six livres two sous—but these are a large parcel——He shook his head——Monsieur *Le Blanc!* Madam *Le Blanc!* did you see any papers of mine?—you maid of the house! run up stairs—*François!* run up after her——

——I must have my remarks——they were the best remarks, cried I, that ever were made—the wisest—the wittiest——What shall I do?—which way shall I turn myself?

Sancho Pança, when he lost his ass's FURNITURE, did not exclaim more bitterly.

James Thurber
The Girls in the Closet 1952

I HAVE reached the age when the strangers I accidentally jostle on sidewalks say, "Sorry, Pop!" instead of "Watch it, Buster!" and the pretty young women I used to help across the perilous streets now snatch me from the path of ten-ton trucks, scold me as if I were their grandpa on one of his bad days, and hurry along with the throng, never giving me another thought. This phenomenon of maturity, this coming of frost and twilight to the autumn rose, would embitter many men, but I take it in my totter. I have learned to embrace middle age, not to wrestle with it, and I accept this considerable difference between forever panting and being constantly short of breath.

The sedentary life imposed by advancing years often leads a man into his past. He sits around the house, going through old scrapbooks and photograph albums, catching glimpses of his younger self, trying to remember the names of the laughing girls in the 1930 snapshots, and arguing with his wife about lost afternoons and forgotten places. One evening, not long ago, with my shawl about my shoulders because of a nasty draught, I got out an album of pictures I had taken with my box Brownie nearly fifteen years ago in Southern France. I came across the strange, obscure snapshot of a telephone, and it whisked me back to the Villa Tamisier, on the French Riviera, where my wife and I spent a tranquil winter before the second World War. I remember that remarkable telephone clearly, possibly because, as in the case of difficult women, I never did figure it out.

We have been in the Villa Tamisier nearly two months before I found out that there was a phone in the house. We didn't need a phone, because we didn't know anybody on the Riviera that season, except Olympy and Maria Sementzoff, who worked for us as gardener and cook. Then one night, about two in the morning, I heard a telephone ringing distantly and realized finally that it was somewhere in the villa itself. I stumbled down the stairs in the dark and followed the sound to the closed door of a small closet. Inside was the telephone, on the floor, snarled up in what appeared to be thirty feet of insulated wire. I took up the receiver and said, "Allo?" and a faraway despairing voice asked me in French if I were Monsieur Duronde in Bruxelles. I explained that he not only had the wrong man but the wrong country and hung up.

"What are you doing down there at this hour of the night?" my wife demanded from her bedroom. I told her I was trying to get a telephone off the floor. She came down, and we worked on the thing together, but the instrument was caught in an obstinate intestinal impaction and we had to leave it where it was. We lit cigarettes and studied the remarkable snarl of wire. My wife finally gave as plausible an explanation as any. She suggested that the owners of the villa, a doctor and his wife who lived in Nice, had probably carried the phone upstairs with them at night to save the cost of a bedroom extension.

"In the end," I put in, "the telephone was gradually imprisoned by the wires, the way an old rowboat is enveloped by morning-glories, and they couldn't get it loose."

My wife took it up from there. "Our landlord, the good doctor, is a fat man," she said, "and obviously couldn't reach the phone, so they had to move away and rent out their villa." I thought this over, "It isn't like the French to be driven from their homes by an lot of wire," I said. She thought *that* over. "Yes, it is," she said, and we went back to bed.

The next day I managed to get the thing loose, and was taking a time exposure of it with my camera when the ample and benign Maria came into the room. Nothing that I did ever surprised Maria. Once she had found me playing boules by myself — boules, as Maria well knew, is a game for two or more players.

On another occasion she came upon me tossing centimes at a small round hole in the center of an iron table on the terrace. She also discovered I labored under the childish delusion that the drawings I kept making could be sold for money.

Olympy and Maria must have spent a lot of time whispering in their quarters at night, trying to figure out the strange Americans. One day she asked me, "Are you paid to stay away from America?" That was the solution she and her husband had arrived at: *persona non grata* in the United States because of my peculiar personal habits, I had sought sanctuary among the tolerant people of France.

"You are photographing the telephone?" Maria asked, interested but not astonished. My French has never been much and my explanation of what I was up to must have sounded something like this: "I am with this telephone and my wife last night because a man has telephoned Bruxelles and we are thinking the doctor is not here because he was too fat to answer the phone." Maria never actually backed away from me, but her eyes in my presence became wary, as if she were watching a man juggling knives. "Is the telephone not extraordinary?" I asked her. She plainly thought I had taken leave of my senses. Since I couldn't think of the French words for wire or length or tangle, I was not able to support my own argument. My wife came downstairs to the rescue, but her French is competent only in dealing with problems of the kitchen, and the three of us merely complicated the situation.

"My husband thinks the doctor is taking the telephone upstairs," said Mrs. Thurber. From Maria's expression it was easy to see that she thought I had found the perfect mate. I lost my patience and began to shout in English, of which Maria understands only one word — "no." "What the hell was the phone doing on the floor in all that wire?" I demanded, *"Je vais chercher* Olympy," said Maria, cautiously, but my wife was determined to solve the situation in French on the spot, having just thought of the word for wire. The word for wire is *fil,* which happens to be very similar to the French word *fille.* So Mrs. Thurber, maintaining an air of tranquillity, said calmly to Maria in French, "There are too many girls in the closet." Maria left to get Olympy, but she didn't come back with him. I think he must have said to her, "Let us wait until they quiet down again. They have these spells, but mercifully they get over them."

Only a few days after the disturbing incident of the telephone, I drove to the movies in Cannes and parked my car on the wrong side of the street, not realizing my mistake until my wife and I came out of the theater. In Cannes, you are supposed to park on one side of the street on even-numbered days of the month, and on the other side on odd-numbered days. We were gratified, but surprised, to find that the windshield of the car had not been posted with an official police summons. I drove back to the Villa Tamisier, eight miles away, over a circuitous route that ended in a secluded nook behind the villa, a private parking lot by no means easy to find.

The next morning, while we were still congratulating ourselves on escaping a ticket, we went out to get into the car, and there, freshly pasted on the windshield, was the police summons with a black X beside "Parking on the even side of a street on an odd-numbered day." We stared at it silently and then my wife said, *"Je vais chercher Maria."*

Well, we got into another one of those three-cornered confusions. To Maria it seemed perfectly reasonable that our car should have been ticketed a day after the offense. Her analysis of the situation went something like this: "The police saw that yours was an American car and so they waited, perhaps in a doorway, and followed you home on motorcycles. It was necessary to find where you live and then to see whether you may not be diplomats or persons of great importance, who could not be arrested without involving the Cannes police and perhaps even the French government in a delicate embarrassment." She had to repeat this several times before we understood it. "How are they finding I am not important?" I asked her, coldly. This was easy for Maria. "They have records," she said, "and they telephone someone in Paris." Apparently it hadn't taken them too long to discover that a 1935 Ford sedan with the license number F-224 belonged to a person unlikely to involve the French government in a *cause célèbre*. I was smart enough to show up for my punishment at police headquarters at Cannes just after lunch the following day, and an amiable sergeant, redolent of wine and Brie, observing that we were innocents who did not know odd from even, or one day from another, let us off with a jolly rebuke and an exchange of compliments. "Ask him who they telephoned in Paris," my wife whispered. I took a stab at it, and the sergeant suddenly exploded into wide gestures and volubility. I think he was telling us how to get from Marseille to Saudi Arabia by ship. When he had finished, we exchanged deep bows, and my wife and I got in the car and started back for the Villa Tamisier. Neither of us said anything for nearly a mile, and then she spoke in her most authoritative tone. "They had run out of windshield stickers," she explained, "and had to go back to headquarters to get some new ones, and when they came back we had driven away."

"Then how did they know the license number of our car?" I demanded.

"They had written it down," said my wife firmly. I laughed at her innocence. "If they forgot to bring stickers," I told her patiently, "they would naturally have forgotten to bring the official notebook in which they write down the license numbers of—"

"Ah, shut up," said my wife.

The other principal problem in France, as seen in the preceding selection, is equally French and equally fastidious: speaking the native language or, more correctly, trying to convince French people to let you try out your high-school Franglais despite the taint to their great and noble tongue. Everything sounds better in French until, of course, we open our mouths or, come to think of it, when many Frenchmen express their not so tender feelings. Remember, though: speaking French can be something more than the ultimate frustration and embarrassment; it can be a lot of fun. Take this anecdote told by the master, Bennett Cerf: "A lady tourist saw her sight-seeing group riding away in a bus without her. After frantically consulting her pocket English-French dictionary, she took off in pursuit, shouting, 'Hey, garçon! Wait! Attendez! Stoppez at once! Je suis gauche derrière!' " And then there's Harriet Beecher Stowe's foolproof method.

Harriet Beecher Stowe
The Steeplechase Method 1854

IN the evening Mrs. C. had her *salon,* a fashion of receiving one's friends on a particular night, that one wishes could be transplanted to American soil.

No invitations are given. It is simply understood that on such an evening, the season through, a lady *receives* her friends. All come that please, without ceremony. A little table is set out with tea and a plate of cake. Behind it presides some fairy Emma or Elizabeth, dispensing tea and talk, bonbons and bon-mots, with equal grace. The guests enter, chat, walk about, spend as much time, or as little, as they choose, and retire. They come when they please, and go when they please, and there is no notice taken of entrée or exit, no time wasted in formal greetings and leave takings.

Up to this hour we had conversed little in French. One is naturally diffident at first; for if one musters courage to commence a conversation with propriety, the problem is how to escape a Scylla in the second and a Charybdis in the third sentence. Said one of our fair entertainers, "When I first began I would think of some sentence till I could say it without stopping, and courageously deliver myself to some guest or acquaintance." But it was like pulling the string of a shower bath. Delighted at my correct sentence, and supposing me *au fait,* they poured upon me such a deluge of French that I held my breath in dismay. Considering, however, that nothing is to be gained by half-way measures, I resolved upon a desperate game. Launching in, I talked away right and left, up hill and down, — jumping over genders, cases, nouns, and adjectives, floundering through swamps and morasses, in a perfect steeple chase of words. Thanks to the proverbial politeness of my friends, I came off covered with glory; the more mistakes I made the more complacent they grew.

"*How many times have I told you children not to play with your food!*"

❧People

❧ *You almost forgot what you came out to the provinces to do: to dis-*
cover who the French really are. But you know that already, don't
you. They're different from Parisians, but similar. They have less to be
gay about, but also less traffic and fewer tourists. They have little in
the way of je nais sais quoi, *but loads of* savoir faire *and* savoir vivre,
as Joseph Barry, an excellent interpreter of all things French, explains.
As with most people and peoples, however, the French are best
described in terms of their contradictions. They are definitely six of
one and a half dozen of the other. To complicate things a bit, the sec-
ond selection consists of the words of an old British major as written
by a Frenchman, Pierre Daninos, and translated into English.

Joseph Barry
La Relaxe 1966

"IN general," French vacationers were asked after one summer holiday, "did you find a lot of people, not so many, or just a few? And
how did you like what you found?"

Half of those who found a lot of people said they like the "animation." Nine out of ten who found only a few people said they pre-
ferred the "calm." It was an ambiguity cleared up by Monsieur
Stoetzel's conclusion: "*Les Parisiens,* more than all the others,
expressed an appreciation for *le calme.* "

It might have been for *la détente* or, as more and more Frenchmen
put it, *la relaxe.* They are passwords to a year-round attitude, twelve
months a year.

The Frenchman, I've already reported, is still resisting the indirect
aggression of an Americanism known as do-it-yourself. If a floor
sags, he walks carefully around it and complains to the landlady. If a
faucet leaks, he dreams of fountains in Spain and lets it go at that. If

the grass grows, he loafs and invites his soul to enjoy the irresistible life force. He no more thinks of cutting it than trimming his own hair.

His wife is a true mate. She does not spur him to be up and doing. She is happy if he is happy. She knows that early to bed and early to rise often means an early grave. In a phrase, she is not ambitious for him and he of course is not ambitious for himself.

In Sweden, I once asked a well-traveled native why his country was so gloomy a paradise. I saw prosperity everywhere, but never a man laughing. (The women, it is said, go to Denmark for husbands.) "We have the American neurosis of ambition," the Swede answered.

In neighboring Norway they do things better. They work much harder in their rugged country, but they sweeten life with more play and purposelessness. They are the Italians of the North (the Italians, according to Cocteau, are good-natured Frenchmen). In summertime, they quit their offices and factories at three or four in the afternoon, eat dinner at five, and take a nap so they are rested and ready for the long twilight nights.

The Frenchman has basically the same approach, but when he can, which is increasingly infrequent—such is the price of prosperity—he breaks his day into digestible halves by dining and reposing for two hours at noon. And he paces himself carefully during the day so that he hasn't given his all by the time the whistle blows. He figures that what is good for him is good for the country.

He arrives at his job precisely on the hour—no sooner, no later. If he were to arrive sooner, he would worry the boss with the spectacle of an employee straining for a better job, which the boss doesn't have for him, since it's his own. If he were to arrive later . . . well, he's glad to have the job he has and would hate to look for another.

Before going home, he stops at a café. The café is his decompression chamber. It prepares him for the low pressure of an evening at home after the high pressure of a day at the office. When he arrives, the children will already have been spanked.

Even the walk home inclines him to relax. The scale of a French city is human. No building rises like a vertical pavement—even in the great city of Paris—to crush him with its height or rob him of the sky. The façades don't compete for his attention and there is a restfulness in the harmonious roofscapes. The streets he takes by choice twist and turn into tree-shaded squares and parks.

But, above all, the Frenchman relaxes because he refuses to take on the idiosyncrasies of others as a personal affront to himself. The

Bohemian or beatnik beards, the bare-toed sandals, the blue jeans worn as a declaration of war against the bourgeoisie are accepted by even the French bourgeois as the natural rights of youth who will settle down, too soon as it is, to a sedate bourgeois life.

Nothing is more relaxing than to live among people who let you be yourself—not as a favor to *you*, but because they want the same freedom for themselves. The French have the virtue of their vice: an individuality so fierce it has produced a dozen political parties and made France almost impossible to govern, yet, at the same time, has produced Paris, the most civilized of cities, and made France the second home of all civilized men. If you personally assume the mission of straightening out your neighbor's morals, behavior, and non-conformist politics, you might as well forget about your peace of mind.

The Frenchman doesn't. He tends to sit high, dry, and skeptical. He is his own measure of all things. His skepticism, he firmly believes, rations his emotions and saves him the fatigue of inevitable disillusion. It is one of his most exasperating, fascinating, stimulating, and astringent traits.

Pierre Daninos
What Is a Frenchman? 1955

IN the secrecy of his Harley Street surgery a friend of mine, a famous brain surgeon, one day opened up an Englishman.

And he discovered: first, one of Her Majesty's battleships, then a waterproof, a royal crown, a cup of tea, a dominion, a policeman, the rules of the Royal and Ancient Golf Club of St. Andrews, a Coldstream Guardsman, a bottle of whisky, a Bible, the Calais-Mediterranean time-table, a Westminster Hospital nurse, a cricket ball, some fog, a bit of the earth on which the sun never sets, and — right at the bottom of his subconscious, lined with age-old turf — a cat-o'-nine-tails and a black-stockinged schoolgirl.

Conscious of having committed an unpardonable indiscretion, rather than appalled by his discovery, he neither called in Scotland Yard nor the Vice Squad: he sewed him up again. And he had to conclude that all those things constitute a really good Englishman. I have often wondered what my friend would find if he cut open a Frenchman.

How should one define a Frenchman?

The accepted definition of the Frenchman as one who eats bread, knows no geography and wears the Legion of Honour in his button-hole, is not inaccurate (although the Legion of Honour when you look more closely is the Order of Ouissam Alaouite).

But it doesn't go far enough.

I am alarmed by the thought that if my friend were to cut open a Frenchman he would fall dizzily into an abyss of contradictions.

Really . . . how can you define these people who spend their Sundays proclaiming that they are republicans and the rest of the week worshipping the Queen of England, who call themselves modest yet always talk about being custodians of the torch of civilization, whose common sense is one of their principal exports, while they keep so little of it for themselves that they overthrow governments almost before they are set up, who keep France in their hearts and their fortunes abroad, who are enemies of Jews in general but intimate friends of some particular Jew, who love to hear their comedians make fun of retired army officers but who brace up at the slightest bugle call, who hate to have their failings exposed but constantly speak ill of themselves, who say they love pure lines but cherish an affection for the Eiffel Tower, who admire the Englishman's ignorance of 'Système D' (the art of wangling) but would think it absurd to declare the correct amount of their incomes to the Inland Revenue, who revel in stories of Scotch meanness but will always try to buy at a price below the marked figure; who refer complacently to their History but don't want any more *histoires,* who loathe crossing a frontier without smuggling some little thing but dislike not keeping the rules, who are anxious to proclaim that you can't take them in but rush to elect a deputy who promises them the moon, who say 'ne'er cast a clout till May is out' but cut off the heating at the end of March, who vaunt the charms of their countryside but let their builders cover it with architectural eyesores, who have a marked respect for the law courts but go to a lawyer only to find out how to get round the law, and finally, who are delighted when a great man talks to them of their *greatness,* their *great* civilizing mission, their *great* country, their *great* traditions, but who dream of retiring after a pleasant *little* life, into a quiet *little* corner, on a *little* piece of ground of their own, with a *little* wife who will be content with inexpensive *little* dresses, concoct for him nice *little* dishes and on occasion invite his friends charmingly to have a *little* game of cards?

These conservatives who for the last two hundred years cease not to slip to the left until they there rediscover their 'right', these republicans who for more than a century have repressed their royalism and taught their children with tears in their eyes the history of the kings who created France — how can a poor devil of an observer define them except in terms of contradictions?

A Frenchman? A being who above all is the opposite of what you think he is.

❧ *The big question remains, the only question of any value to the humorist: do the French have a sense of humor? Do they have* savoir rire? *Or are we just too dense, or illiterate, to get their jokes? A debate of sorts is held below between two very funny men, Laurence Sterne and Donald Moffat, writing nearly two centuries apart.*

Laurence Sterne
Character 1768

AND how do you find the French? said the Count de B——, after he had given me the Passport.

The reader may suppose, that after so obliging a proof of courtesy, I could not be at a loss to say something handsome to the inquiry.

Mais passe, pour cela; Speak frankly, said he: do you find all the urbanity in the French which the world give us the honour of? I had found every thing, I said, which confirmed it. *Vraiment,* said the Count; *les François sont polis.* To an excess, replied I.

The Count took notice of the word *excesse;* and would have it I meant more than I said. I defended myself a long time as well as I could against it; he insisted I had a reserve, and that I would speak my opinion frankly.

I believe, Mons. le Count, said I, that man has a certain compass, as well as an instrument; and that the social and other calls have occasion by turns for every key in him; so that if you begin a note too high or too low, there must be a want either in the upper or under part, to fill up the system of harmony. The Count de B—— did not understand music, so desired me to explain it some other way. A polish'd nation, my dear Count, said I, makes every one its debtor; and besides, urbanity itself, like the fair sex, has so many charms, it goes against the heart to say it can do ill; and yet, I believe, there is but a certain line of perfection, that man, take him altogether, is impower'd to arrive at—if he gets beyond, he rather exchanges qualities than gets them. I must not presume to say, how far this has affected the French in the subject we are speaking of, but should it ever be the case of the English, in the progress of their refinements, to arrive at the same polish which distinguishes the French, if we did not lose the *politesse du cœur,* which inclines men more to humane actions, than courteous ones, we should at least lose that distinct variety and originality of character, which distinguishes them, not only from each other, but from all the world besides.

I had a few of King William's shillings as smooth as glass in my pocket; and foreseeing they would be of use in the illustration of my hypothesis, I had got them into my hand, when I had proceeded so far.

See, Mons. le Count, said I, rising up, and laying them before him upon the table; by jingling and rubbing one against another for seventy years together in one body's pocket or another's, they are become so much alike, you can scarce distinguish one shilling from another.

The English, like ancient medals, kept more apart, and passing but few people's hands, preserve the first sharpnesses which the fine hand of Nature has given them: they are not so pleasant to feel, but, in return, the legend is so visible, that at the first look you see whose image and superscription they bear. But the French, Mons. le Count, added I (wishing to soften what I had said), have so many excellencies, they can the better spare this: they are a loyal, a gallant, a generous, an ingenious, and good-temper'd people as is under heaven; if they have a fault, they are too *serious*.

Mon Dieu! cried the Count, rising out of his chair.

Mais vous plaisantez, said he, correcting his exclamation. I laid my hand upon my breast, and with earnest gravity assured him it was my most settled opinion.

The Count said he was mortified he could not stay to hear my reasons, being engaged to go that moment to dine with the Duc de C——.

But if it is not too far to come to Versailles to eat your soup with me, I beg, before you leave France, I may have the pleasure of knowing you retract your opinion, or, in what manner you support it. But if you do support it, Mons. Anglois, said he, you must do it with all your powers, because you have the whole world against you.

Donald Moffat
Poisson d'Avril 1937

"HUMOR?" said Mr. Marshall. "They haven't any, in our sense. They have wit, which suits them better."

Mr. Marshall, up from Orne for the day, had met Mr. Mott for lunch, and they were indulging in their favorite pastime — over some oysters and a glass of wine — of dissecting the French character. The little café was crowded; they were squeezed at a small table between a party of four men of business who were swiftly absorbing snails stewed in garlic, and talking as one man about *les affaires,* and, on the other side, a stout middle-aged man of obviously provincial origin who was seriously putting away the most enormous meal Mr. Mott had ever seen consumed outside the zoo. Mr. Marshall had to raise his voice to be heard above the clatter of dishes, the hurrying waiters, and the roar of autobuses and taxis outside the open door of the restaurant.

"And their favorite dish," Mr. Marshall resumed, spearing an oyster, "is irony. Irony is the pudding, wit the plums. Conversation in France is a highly skilled game, with rules which everyone knows from infancy. It's a fine art, polished, conventionalized, and played for its own sake. It sounds as if everyone talked at once, the ball is tossed about so quickly; but they don't, really. What they look for in conversation is wit. It should be epigrammatic, and scholarly if possible, but ironic in any case. The Frenchman likes to imply, with an allusive rapier, not bang out facts with a bludgeon. Monologues — like this — not allowed."

"I think I'd like it, then," said Mr. Mott. They were really old friends.

"No you wouldn't. It's very tiring, till you're used to it." Mr. Marshall took up his glass and drained his wine at a gulp, then filled it again. Mr. Mott said nothing.

"But humor," Mr. Marshall went on — "no, no! The essence of a sense of humor is the ability to laugh at oneself — and other things that ought to be taken seriously. Life is a serious business in France. The responsibility of being a Frenchman is no joke. He finds plenty of objects to laugh at, of course, but his own hopes and ambitions and other little gods of the kind are not among them. However witty he may be when a Stavisky robs the State, — and there were some lovely pieces coined at the time, — he is not amused when he himself loses money, or when he is accidentally deprived of his dinner. Therefore, I say, he has no sense of humor, in our meaning."

"Well," said Mr. Mott, "I won't argue the point. No doubt you're right. Anyway, you can't generalize about such things."

"Here's another point of distinction: we like the kind of humor that leaves something to the imagination. Say all you like about the typical French epigram —"

"I haven't said a word about it," Mr. Mott interrupted. "Want some coffee?"

"Yes . . . The Frenchman likes it fully rounded, complete, no tails left hanging adrift. The story-teller must supply the answer, not, as with us, the imagination of the tellee. I saw something in *Punch* a while ago — a drawing of a vast, trackless plain, empty of everything except a man on a motorcycle leaning over another man on the ground, evidently a pedestrian he has just knocked down. And the motorcyclist is saying: 'But surely, sir, you heard me sound my horn.' I don't believe that the average Frenchman would be much amused. He'd be waiting for the other's retort — presumably witty — to round it off. But, as you say, it's hard to generalize. I wish I had a typical Frenchman here to try it out on."

"He's right beside you," said Mr. Mott, "if ever I saw one."

They both glanced at the solitary provincial at the next table, who had reached the salad stage. His method of eating salad was to poke a bit of lettuce between his lips, then ram the rest of it home with his fork — an oily business, but evidently satisfactory. "Moreover," continued Mr. Mott with malice, "if you had an ounce of courage you would try it out on him."

Mr. Marshall thought for a moment, and presently stole another glance at the absorbed and devoted archetype. "Why not?" he said presently. "Let's wait till he's finished, then ask him to join us for a brandy. Do we bet the usual?"

"Ten francs? All right. Try him on a French story first."

"Yes. That bicycle story's a bit hard, for ice breaking. Let me think, now." And Mr. Marshall thought to such good purpose that their oblivious neighbor had no more than finished his third peach from the dish of fruit before him when Mr. Marshall murmured, "I've got it: a French classic, *poisson d'avril!*" — a phrase that to Mr. Mott was devoid of meaning. Fish of April? What rot, he thought.

The Frenchman was surprised at their invitation, but charmed to join them. He introduced himself as M. Burton, up from Tours for a day's business. The waiter served them liqueurs, and they talked of food and wine, the restaurants of Paris and of Tours, and presently, the fine spring weather having been mentioned, Mr. Marshall said: —

"Apropos of nothing in particular, monsieur, I wonder if it is the custom in France, as it is with us, to celebrate the first of April with little jokes at the expense of one's friends?"

"But naturally, monsieur — *poisson d'avril,*" said the other, smiling. "I will confess that for one moment I thought that your invitation might be in the nature of such a jest."

Polite and amused disclaimers from Mr. Mott and Mr. Marshall.

"It is interesting nevertheless," continued Mr. Marshall, "to speculate on the origin of such customs. In our country, when the joke suc-
ceeds, we cry 'April Fool' at the victim; and you, 'Poisson d'avril.' I
wonder if you can tell us how the fish ever found itself in that pond?"

"Alas, no," replied M. Burton. "When I was a boy my grand-
mother used to say that the April jokes were always played during
the spring festival when the new wine of the previous autumn was
first tasted; and of course it is the day on which deceived husbands
usually find it convenient to remain indoors. But as to how the fish
crept in — that I do not know."

"You remind me of an anecdote I read in the paper the other day,
surely the classic example of the April jest — the story of the little girl
and her mother. Do you know it?"

"Not I, monsieur; pray proceed."

"Very well, then. It seems," Mr. Marshall began slowly, "that
Mamma is lying in bed in a half doze, this particular April morning,
and the sun, peeping through the blinds to caress her smiling lips and
touch her sleepy eyelids with its gentle warmth, gives her assurance
that the day is fine. She feels happy. Papa, good man, has presumably left for his office, and she will not see him again till he comes
home for lunch. Lucille, the new and pretty parlormaid, has doubtless already donned the traditional short skirt and frilly apron of her
calling, and is about her household duties, which consist of whisk-
ing a feather duster over the mantelpiece in the salon and breaking
into the wistful but naughty songs of her native village. I do not bore
you, monsieur?"

"Not at all, my friend. I have never yet had the good fortune to
meet such a parlormaid in France, it is true, but —"

"Nor have I, monsieur. I fear that she exists only upon the musi-
cal-comedy stage; but as this is comedy, I thought I might take the
liberty of expressing — However. The maid is dusting the parlor, and
Marie-Thérèse, Mamma's little daughter and her greatest treasure,
would by this time, thinks Mamma, be spraying her dollies with
their morning perfume. Mamma, as I have said, feels happy. She
wonders if Bertrand really meant what his eyes proclaimed when he
pressed her knee behind the palms last night, at the reception of
Madame la Duchesse de Milletonnerre. Mamma sighs tenderly and,
opening her eyes, reaches for her mirror and gives herself over to her
favorite occupation.

"At this moment a clamor arises at the door, and in rushes the little
Marie-Thérèse, a rosy finger at her lip, on her innocent countenance
a look of intense excitement. Mamma, her heart aflutter with tender

forebodings, rises on one elbow, and, 'Marie-Thérèse, my little one, my treasure, what is the matter? Speak, I implore thee!' she cries.

" '*Ah, maman,*' piteously answers the little one, 'I come from peeping into the chamber of Lucille, meaning to place a bouquet of flowers at her window to surprise her, and there I found that all is not as it should be — that Lucille, in fact, is still in her bed.'

" 'Lucille in her bed at this hour?' cries the mother. *'Quelle horreur!* And didst thou then enter, my treasure, to see if perchance she has been stricken with a malady?'

" '*Ah, non, maman,* I started to enter, when to my astonishment I perceived that Lucille was not alone in her bed, but that by her side reposed the figure of another — the figure of a man, a stranger. I silently withdrew, unseen, to speed to thee with the news of this irregularity.'

"At these tidings Mamma springs from her bed, her lovely eyes distended with anger, flings a pink satin wrap about her white shoulders, and, followed by the little Marie-Thérèse (across whose lips a mischievous smile might have been seen to steal), swiftly mounts the stairs to the chamber of the good-for-nothing Lucille, her anger rising as she goes. They reach the landing and pause beside the door of the faithless one, while Mamma whispers to her little daughter, 'Stay back, my child, while I enter suddenly and surprise this guilty baggage and the stranger in her arms.'

"She advances, she throws wide the door. Her eyes assure her that the little Marie-Thérèse has exaggerated the situation in no particular.

"But what is it that she now hears, as the guilty couple retreat with presence of mind beneath the coverlet? It is the little Marie-Thérèse, who dances round the room and claps her hands at the success of her innocent prank, shouting in childish glee:—

" '*Poisson d'avril! C'est papa!*' "

M. Burton laughed heartily, as Mr. Marshall and Mr. Mott anxiously watched him. "Well told, monsieur," he said at length, "so well told that I did not wish to admit to you that it is not, after all, new to me. I enjoy your English humor, monsieur, and this story in particular has always seemed to me the classic example of it."

He got up to go, thanking them warmly for their hospitality.

"Which seems to leave us," said Mr. Mott, smiling, "just about where we started. Except," he added, holding out his hand, "for the little matter of ten francs?"

*It is hard to know anyone, much less a foreigner, that is, someone
fluent only in a language we can at best muddle through. So why
bother trying? It's twice as much fun simply to imagine whatever you
will, as Robert Louis Stevenson does in the following piece. (Note that
Stevenson is leading a donkey.)*

Robert Louis Stevenson
Nothing 1879

A VERY old shepherd, hobbling on a pair of sticks, and wearing a
black cap of liberty, as if in honor of his nearness to the grave,
directed me to the road for *St. Germain de Calberte.* There was
something solemn in the isolation of this infirm and ancient creature. Where he dwelt, how he got upon this high ridge, or how he
proposed to get down again, were more than I could fancy. Not far
off upon my right was the famous *Plan de Font Morte,* where *Poul*
with his Armenian sabre slashed down the Camisards of *Séguier.*
This, methought, might be some *Rip van Winkle* of the war, who
had lost his comrades, fleeing before *Poul,* and wandered ever since
upon the mountains. It might be news to him that *Cavalier* had surrendered, or *Roland* had fallen fighting with his back against an
olive. And while I was thus working on my fancy, I heard him hailing
in broken tones, and saw him waiving me to come back with one of
two sticks. I had already got some way past him; but, leaving
Modestine once more, retraced my steps.

Alas, it was a very commonplace affair. The old gentleman had
forgot to ask the pedler what he sold, and wished to remedy this
neglect.

I told him sternly, 'Nothing.'

'Nothing?' cried he.

I repeated 'Nothing,' and made off.

It's odd to think of, but perhaps I thus became as inexplicable to
the old man as he had been to me.

*The peculiarity we most often ascribe to the French is strange eating
habits, their love for things like snails, truffles, and frogs. No one has
any trouble imagining the capture of a snail — which has less chance
of getting away than a pig in a poke — and everyone knows you have
to* chercher les truffles, *but how do they catch frogs? The way we
used to when we were kids? They'd end up being pretty expensive,*

especially since they throw away everything but the legs. Here's the way they do it, or did it way back when.

James St. John
Frog-Fishing 1788

THERE are many persons who cannot believe that the French eat frogs, but I assure you it is a fact that they do. There are persons who make it their business to catch them; and they are sold by the hundred in the markets. In a book describing the diversions used in France, such as angling, shooting, catching larks by looking-glasses, &c. I have seen *la pêche de grenouilles,* or frog-fishing, particularly mentioned. To catch the frogs, the fishermen put one of them into a glass vessel which he dips into a brook. On which the creature, finding itself in so strange a situation, confined in the midst of water in a transparent machine, or I may say invisible prison, begins to croak most melodiously, and by his croaking makes great multitudes of other frogs come to him on every side, as if to rescue their companion: then the frog-fisher valiantly seizes on his prey. As frogs are accounted fish in France, the people are permitted to eat them upon Fridays. And all declare, that a *fricassée* of frogs *à la sauce blanche,* is quite delicious; and frogs are often seen on the very genteelest tables in the kingdom. The hindquarters of the frogs are the only parts that are eaten or served at table. A French person said to me, that he did not think we censured them with justice for eating frogs while we continued to eat shrimps and cockles, which appeared to him as animals much more contemptibly small, and not so delicious as frogs.

&For centuries, as no less than Nathaniel Hawthorne will attest, the French have been known to prefer multicourse meals that leave mere mortals famished; in other words, the cuisine's not so nouvelle: "I doubt whether English cookery, for the very reason that it is so simple, is not better for men's moral and spiritual nature than French. In the former case, you know that you are gratifying your animal needs and propensities, and are duly ashamed of it; but, in dealing with these French delicacies, you delude yourself into the idea that you are cultivating your taste while satisfying your appetite. This last, however, it requires a good deal of perseverance to accomplish."

Of all the foods France is famous for, French bread is the one most often and lovingly encountered, especially by young tourists, who *exist on it and Camembert alone. The croissant may be the lightest, crumbliest, most delectable baked good in the land, but the baguette is an institution, and the French love nothing more than an institution.*

Art Buchwald
It's All in the Crust 1961

WHAT is the secret of French bread? This is the question that Mrs. Margaret Rudkin, president of Pepperidge Farm, the largest independent bakery in the United States, has been studying since she's been coming to Paris for the past thirty-seven years.

"The secret," Mrs. Rudkin said, "is the freshness of the crust. The French will go to the bakery three times a day to get fresh bread. Americans prefer to go once a week and keep their bread in the freezer. When you go mad over French bread, you're going mad over the crust, which has a wonderful rich flavor as well as terrific eye appeal. French bread holds its flavor because it is sold unsliced and stays fresh longer.

"In the United States we're not allowed to sell unwrapped bread, and for this reason we can't get the crispness in our bread that the French do. When bread is wrapped, the moisture in the package, which can't escape, softens the crust, and we can't ever hope to have our crusts as fresh.

"The other thing, I think, that makes French bread so good is the holes in it. Americans refuse to accept holes in their bread — the French seem to like the holes. I find even the holes in French bread taste good."

But Mrs. Rudkin said that if she could develop a bread with holes in it she thinks diet-conscious Americans might finally go for it. "Those who are worried about their weight could say they're eating holes and not bread, and those who feel there is not enough nourishment in the bread could fill the holes with peanut butter."

Mrs. Rudkin whetted my appetite to find out more about French bread.

I found out French bread is to the Frenchman what the umbrella is to the Englishman. It is carried at all times, rain or shine, and has many functions. You can hail a taxi with French bread, use it to tap someone on the back when you want to get off a bus or to get a cat off the vegetables, and wave it when General de Gaulle drives by.

There are many types of French bread. The very, very thin long loaf is called "la ficelle," which means "the thread." The ficelle is mostly crust with very light dough inside. It naturally breaks very easily. Because of its thinness the ends are very pointed, and it must be handled more like a rapier than a saber.

The ficelle is excellent for sticking out of the car window when you want to make a right turn, and for pointing out places of interest to foreigners.

The next size is "la baguette" (the stick), which is the most popular size. The baguette is carried like a rifle, the butt of the bread in the palm of your hand and the other end across the shoulder. When meeting your boss or your wife on the street you present arms, holding the loaf vertically in front of you six inches from the top and bottom. In cases where people have suffered ski accidents it can also be used as a cane.

It is bad form to twirl the baguette or swing it like a baseball bat in the street.

Shorter and thicker than the baguette is "le bâtard" (which means what you think it does). The bâtard is a cross between the baguette and the "pain fantaisie" (fancy bread, which isn't very fancy). The bâtard is excellent for political demonstrations and carrying late at night in case of attack.

The "gros pain," or big bread, is as long as the baguette and as thick as the bâtard. It is chiefly bought by large families, but, because it is so unwieldly, the mother sends all the children to buy it. They usually carry it home like a ladder.

The French bakers, unfortunately, have been trying to imitate American sliced bread, but because it serves no use other than to be eaten, sliced bread in France hasn't been very successful.

The French love food. They've made an art out of the prehistoric urge to do more than simply survive. But they love their food, their vegetables, their breads, their meats and game. When they think of foreign food, they feel surrounded by barbarians, by Spanish rice, Italian sausage, German beer, and English muffins. Here is an anecdote to give you a better picture of French xenogourmophobia, by Frances Trollope, mother of the British novelist Anthony Trollope and most famous for making the young United States the laughingstock of Britain.

Frances Trollope
Taste Something *1836*

WE have been on a regular shopping tour this morning, which was finished by our going into an English pastry-cook's to eat buns. While thus engaged, we amused ourselves by watching the proceedings of a French party, who entered also for the purpose of making a morning goûter upon cakes.

They had all of them more or less the air of having fallen upon a terra incognita, showing many indications of surprise at sight of the ultra-marine compositions which appeared before them; but there was a young man of the party who, it was evident, had made up his mind to quiz without measure all the foreign dainties that the shop afforded, evidently considering their introduction as a very unjustifiable interference with the native manufacture.

"Est-il possible!" said he, with an air of grave and almost indignant astonishment, as he watched a lady of his party preparing to eat an English bun, — "Est-il possible that you can prefer these strange-looking comestibles à la pâtisserie française?"

"Mais goûtez-en," said the lady, presenting a specimen of the same kind as that she was herself eating: "ils sont excellens."

"No, no! it is enough to look at them!" said her cavalier, almost shuddering. "There is no lightness, no elegance, no grace in any single gâteau here."

"Mais goûtez quelque chose," reiterated the lady.

"Vous le voulez absolument!" exclaimed the young man; "quelle tyrannie! . . . and what a proof of obedience I am about to give you! . . . Voyons donc!" he continued, approaching a plate on which were piled some truly English muffins, which, as you know, are of a somewhat mysterious manufacture, and about as palatable if eaten untoasted as a slice from a leathern glove. To this *gâteau,* as he supposed it to be, the unfortunate connoisseur in pâtisserie approached, exclaiming with rather a theatrical air, "Voilà donc ce que je vais faire pour vos beaux yeux!"

As he spoke, he took up one of the pale tough things, and, to our extreme amusement, attempted to eat it. Any one might be excused for making a few grimaces on such an occasion, and a Frenchman's privilege in this line is well known; but this hardy experimentalist outdid this privilege. He was in a perfect agony, and his spittings and reproachings were so vehement, that friends, strangers, boutiquier, and all, even down to a little befloured urchin who entered at the moment with a tray of patties, burst into uncontrollable laughter, which the unfortunate, to do him justice, bore with extreme good humour, only making his fair countrywoman promise that she would never insist upon his eating English confectionary again.

&*That's enough about our need to know and understand the French. Let's take a look at you (oh, not again) and me, at us, he who the French (and we ourselves at that) love to hate: the tourist. He's the one you'll end up eating with and sharing dooble-vay-says with; in fact, you might even be married to or otherwise involved with one. Though their population density in the provinces is not what it is in Paris, the tourist is still everywhere, on every beach, at every restaurant, climbing every mountain, Fording every stream in his rental Escort (please distinguish this from his rented escort, something hard to find outside Paris). Humorists are attracted to tourists the way tourists are attracted to souvenirs or, more precisely, the way flies are attracted to — no, not what you think — French restaurants. Below, A. J. Liebling and Mark Twain get in their licks with the old swatter.*

A. J. Liebling
American Incubi 1958

IN the evening, in the restaurant of the Hôtel Poularde, a shrill American couple arrived with three specimen demons from a breeding farm by Hieronymus Bosch. They had apparently crept in and out of the woman's womb and convinced her they were human children. All, the woman recited in a monotonous imitation of a train whistle, had been on the road all day, coming from Paris. They probably had tried to do the Château district on the way. It was nine o'clock and she demanded that her children be fed instantly. The children saw a large *langouste,* whose fiery hue possibly reminded them of their last pre-earthly habitat. They screamed that they wanted for their supper "lobster," and the mother shouted that they never liked lobster, reminding them how they had spewed it out at Dinard, and how deathly sick it had made them at Plymouth. The father said what the hell was the use, let them have lobster, but not cold. They wanted it broiled. *The maître d'hôtel* had learned his English in England — he might have understood "grilled," but broiled stopped him — and the woman screamed that none of these stinkers could understand English, that "they" had sworn in Paris that this was a good hotel, and here were her little children starving to death. The director of the hotel came and understood that they wanted hot lobster — it would demand thirty minutes, he said. Nothing else would do.

The children, waiting, screamed continually, and one of them lay under the table, kicking his father's shins. The director of the hotel suggested the permissive pair remove the children from the dining room; he would serve the hot lobster, which he of course realized they would reject in some disgusting manner, in their living quarters. At that, the woman went off her chump completely. I left, and when I returned at midnight, after a discreet patrol of the hermit crabs' bars, I heard the woman howling still, in her bedroom, that she would not stay the night in a hotel where they insulted her li'l children. Her husband, I judged from the cadence of her howls, was slugging her by now, and I went to sleep hoping he would kill her, strangle the incubi and commit suicide.

Mark Twain
The Old Travelers 1869

THEY say they do not have accidents on these French roads, and I think it must be true. If I remember rightly, we passed high above wagon roads, or through tunnels under them, but never crossed them on their own level. About every quarter of a mile, it seemed to me, a man came out and held up a club till the train went by, to signify that every thing was safe ahead. Switches were changed a mile in advance, by pulling a wire rope that passed along the ground by the rail, from station to station. Signals for the day and signals for the night gave constant and timely notice of the position of switches.

No, they have no railroad accidents to speak of in France. But why? Because when one occurs, *somebody* has to hang for it. They go on the principle that it is better that one innocent man should suffer than five hundred. Not hang, may be, but be punished at least with such vigor of emphasis as to make negligence a thing to be shuddered at by railroad officials for many a day thereafter. "No blame attached to the officers" — that lying and disaster-breeding verdict so common to our soft-hearted juries, is seldom rendered in France. If the trouble occurred in the conductor's department, that officer must suffer if his subordinate can not be proven guilty; if in the engineer's department, and the case be similar, the engineer must answer.

The Old Travelers — those delightful parrots who have "been here before," and know more about the country than Louis Napoleon knows now or ever will know — tell us these things, and we believe them because they are pleasant things to believe, and because they are plausible and savor of the rigid subjection to law and order which we behold about us everywhere.

But we love the Old Travelers. We love to hear them prate, and drivel and lie. We can tell them the moment we see them. They always throw out a few feelers; they never cast themselves adrift till they have sounded every individual and know that he has not traveled. Then they open their throttle-valves, and how they do brag, and sneer, and swell, and soar, and blaspheme that sacred name of Truth! Their central idea, their grand aim, is to subjugate you, keep you down, make you feel insignificant and humble in the blaze of their cosmopolitan glory! They will not let you know anything. They sneer at your most inoffensive suggestions; they laugh unfeelingly at your treasured dreams of foreign lands; they brand the statements of your traveled aunts and uncles as the stupidest absurdities; they deride your most trusted authors and demolish the fair images they have set up for your willing worship with the pitiless ferocity of the fanatic iconoclast! But still I love the Old Travelers. I love them for their witless platitudes; for their supernatural ability to bore; for their delightful asinine vanity; for their luxuriant fertility of imagination; for their startling, their brilliant, their overwhelming mendacity!

Drawing Close To The Edge

*F*our strangers disguised in simple blue and white, evidently wishing to escape observation. The shortest and fairest of the four (a foreigner by his accent) nodding to the country maidens, heedless of the remonstrances of his companions. No; he will not be restrained. He seizes his pencil, and insists on having that dear little Norman face in the wonderful cap. Scowl of jealous lover at Don Juan. Angry murmur among the crowd. They dash their beards with lemonade, and advance threateningly. Situation critical! The three in despair! Ah, happy inspiration! They touch (with simple grace) their foreheads significantly — smile mysteriously at the crowd, and glance at the reckless artist. The gentle superstition still lingers among the villagers, of reverence for such affliction — he is saved! The portrait is presented to the appeased lover, who, scornful of expense, at once orders *eau sucrée* for the company. General reconciliation — village dance in *sabots* — chorus! — *J. L. Molloy, c1910*

"... and then, somewhere between Vieux-Certan and Vouvray, we found this
super little drying-out clinic ..."

❧Return

❧France does not end at its borders. It may last forever, in your heart or in your stomach; it may reappear on special, or inappropriate, occasions; it may vanish slowly, like a mint or, as in the next piece, by one of Britain's most humorous, Max Beerbohm, it may disappear in an instant. Sometimes, as in the final piece, by Canada's favorite son Stephen Leacock, it invades the tranquillity of the living room distorted into boorish stories and out-of-focus slide-shows.

Max Beerbohm
A Home-Coming 1923

BELIKE, returning from a long pilgrimage, in which you have seen many strange men and strange cities, and have had your imagination stirred by marvellous experiences, you have never, at the very end of your journey, almost in sight of your home, felt suddenly that all you had been seeing and learning was as naught — a pack of negligible illusions, faint and forgotten. From me, however, this queer sensation has not been withheld. It befell me a few days ago; in a cold grey dawn, and in the Buffet of Dover Harbour.

I had spent two months far away, wandering and wondering; and now I had just fulfilled two thirds of the little tripartite journey from Paris to London. I was sleepy, as one always is after that brief and twice broken slumber. I was chilly, for is not the dawn always bleak at Dover, and perforated always with a bleak and drizzling rain? I was sad, for I had watched from the deck the white cliffs of Albion coming nearer and nearer to me, towering over me, and in the familiar drizzle looking to me more than ever ghastly for that I had been so long and so far away from them. Often though that harsh, chalky coast had thus borne down on me, I had never yet felt so exactly and lamentably like a criminal arrested on an extradition warrant.

In its sleepy, chilly shell my soul was still shuddering and whimpering. Piteously it conjured me not to take it back into this cruel humdrum. It rose up and fawned on me. 'Down, Sir, down!' said I sternly. I pointed out to it that needs must when the devil drives, and that it ought to think itself a very lucky soul for having had two happy, sunny months of fresh and curious adventure. 'A sorrow's crown of sorrow,' it murmured, 'is remembering happier things.' I declared the sentiment to be as untrue as was the quotation trite, and told my soul that I looked keenly forward to the pleasure of writing, in collaboration with it, that book of travel for which I had been so sedulously amassing notes and photographs by the way.

This colloquy was held at a table in the Buffet. I was sorry, for my soul's sake, to be sitting there. Britannia owns nothing more crudely and inalienably Britannic than her Buffets. The barmaids are but incarnations of her own self, thinly disguised. The stale buns and the stale sponge-cakes must have been baked, one fancies, by her own heavy hand. Of her everything is redolent. She it is that has cut the thick stale sandwiches, bottled the bitter beer, brewed the unpalatable coffee. Cold and hungry though I was, one sip of this coffee was one sip too much for me. I would not mortify my body by drinking more of it, although I had to mortify my soul by lingering over it till one of the harassed waiters would pause to be paid for it. I was somewhat comforted by the aspect of my fellow-travellers at the surrounding tables. Dank, dishevelled, dismal, they seemed to be resenting as much as I the return to the dear home-land. I suppose it was the contrast between them and him that made me stare so hard at the large young man who was standing on the threshold and surveying the scene.

He looked, as himself would undoubtedly have said, 'fit as a fiddle,' or 'right as rain.' His cheeks were rosy, his eyes sparkling. He had his arms akimbo, and his feet planted wide apart. His grey bowler rested on the back of his head, to display a sleek coating of hair plastered down over his brow. In his white satin tie shone a dubious but large diamond, and there was the counter-attraction of geraniums and maidenhair-fern in his button-hole. So fresh was the nosegay that he must have kept it in water during the passage! Or perhaps these vegetables had absorbed by mere contact with his tweeds the subtle secret of his own immarcescibility. I remembered now that I had seen him, without realising him, on the platform of the Gare du Nord. 'Gay Paree' was still written all over him. But evidently he was no repiner.

Unaccountable though he was, I had no suspicion of what he was about to do. I think you will hardly believe me when I tell you what he did. 'A traveller's tale' you will say, with a shrug. Yet I swear to you that it is the plain and solemn truth. If you still doubt me, you have the excuse that I myself hardly believed the evidence of my eyes. In the Buffet of Dover Harbour, in the cold grey dawn, in the brief interval between boat and train, the large young man, shooting his cuffs, strode forward, struck a confidential attitude across the counter, and began to flirt with the barmaid.

Open-mouthed, fascinated, appalled, I watched this monstrous and unimaginable procedure. I was not near enough to overhear what was said. But I knew by the respective attitudes that the time-honoured ritual was being observed strictly by both parties. I could see the ice of haughty indifference thawing, little by little, under the fire of gallant raillery. I could fix the exact moment when 'Indeed?' became 'I daresay,' and when 'Well, I *must* say' gave place to 'Go along,' and when 'Oh, *I* don't mind you — not particularly' was succeeded by 'Who gave you them flowers?' . . . All in the cold grey dawn . . .

The cry of 'Take your places, please!' startled me into realisation that all the other passengers had vanished. I hurried away, leaving the young man still in the traditional attitude which he had assumed from the first — one elbow sprawling on the counter, one foot cocked over the other. My porter had put my things into a compartment exactly opposite the door of the Buffet. I clambered in.

Just as the guard blew his whistle, the young man or monster came hurrying out. He winked at me. I did not return his wink.

I suppose I really ought to have raised my hat to him. Pre-eminently, he was one of those who have made England what it is. But they are the very men whom one does not care to meet just after long truancy in other lands. He was the backbone of the nation. But ought backbones to be exposed?

Though I would rather not have seen him then and there, I did realise, nevertheless, the overwhelming interest of him. I knew him to be a stranger sight, a more memorable and instructive, than any of the fair sights I had been seeing. He made them all seem nebulous and unreal to me. Beside me lay my despatch-box. I unlocked it, drew from it all the notes and all the photographs I had brought back with me. These, one by one, methodically, I tore up, throwing their fragments out of the window, not grudging them to the wind.

Stephen Leacock
The People Just Back from Europe Who Never Should Have Left Home 1928

"Y ES," said my hostess as she poured me out a cup of tea, "we're back from Europe."

"You were there some time, were you not?" I asked.

"We were on the Continent all summer," she said; "we had a perfectly glorious time!"

"How did you like Paris?" I asked.

"Fine. There were some people from Kentucky in the same hotel with us — the Johnsons from Louisville, perhaps you know them — and we went round with them all the time; and of course we got to know a lot of other Americans through the steamship company and through the hotels and like that."

"The French," I said, "are so easy and agreeable to meet, are they not?"

"Oh, yes, indeed, we met people from all over — from Maine, and from Chicago and from the Middle West, and quite a lot of Southern people, too. In fact we were quite a cosmopolitan crowd."

"Very much so," I said, "and did you see much of the monuments and the historical things around Paris?"

"Just about everything, I imagine," my hostess replied with animation. "There was an American gentleman from Decatur, Indiana — I think he's professor of French in the Baptist College there — and he took us all round and told us all about everything. He showed us Washington's Monument in the big square and Benjamin Franklin and that tablet there is — perhaps you've seen it — to President McKinley — oh, yes, indeed, we saw everything."

"Of course you saw the pictures ——"

"Oh, certainly. There's just a lovely picture done this year by a young girl from the art school in Omaha and they've got it hung up right there in the annual exhibition. We thought it the best thing there."

"I'm sure you did," I said, "and I suppose you liked the restaurants and the French cooking?"

"We did indeed, and, say, we found the cutest little place — it's in the Roo something or other, near that big church where the American Legion went — and they have everything done in real American style. My husband said you couldn't get a better steak in Chicago

190

than what they had there, and they had pancakes and waffles with maple syrup. Really, as we all agreed, we might just as well have been at home."

☙ *Well, as they say in France,* c'est tout, *roughly translatable as "that's all, folks" or "the jig is up." On behalf of all the humorists, travel writers, and cartoonists who have taken France on, win, lose, or draw, I wish you* bon voyage, bon chance, bon appétit, *and a host of other* bon-bons. Bon soir.

Acknowledgments

MAX BEERBOHM: By permission of Mrs. Eva Reichmann. LUDWIG BEMELMANS: Used by permission of International Creative Management. Copyright 1948 by Ludwig Bemelmans. ROBERT C. BENCHLEY: "The French, They Are—" from *My Ten Years in a Quandary and How They Grew.* Copyright 1936 by Robert C. Benchley. Renewed 1964 by Gertrude Benchley. "Route Nationale 14" from *Benchley or Else.* Copyright 1947 by Robert C. Benchley. Both reprinted by permission of Harper & Row, Publishers, Inc. HEYWOOD BROUN: Permission granted by Bill Cooper Associates, Inc. on behalf of Heywood Broun. ART BUCHWALD: Reprinted with permission of the author. ALAN COREN: Reproduced by permission of *Punch.* HART CRANE: Reprinted with permission of the Rare Book and Manuscript Library, Columbia University. PIERRE DANINOS: Reprinted from *Major Thompson Lives in France,* trans. Robin Farn, Jonathan Cape, © 1955, by permission of Georges Borchardt, Inc. GEOFFREY DICKINSON: Reproduced by permission of *Punch.* MARGARET FISHBACK: Reprinted by permission; © 1927, 1955 The New Yorker Magazine, Inc. FORD MADOX FORD: From *A Mirror to France.* Copyright © renewed 1954 by Janice Biala. WALTER GOETZ: Reprinted from Pierre Daninos, *Major Thompson Lives in France,* Jonathan Cape, © 1955, by permission of Georges Borchardt, Inc. RUBE GOLDBERG AND SAM BOAL: Reprinted from *Rube Goldberg's Guide to Europe,* by Rube Goldberg and Sam Boal, by permission of Vanguard Press, Inc. Copyright © 1954, by Rube Goldberg and Sam Boal. Renewed © 1982 by Irma Goldberg and Sam Boal. JAN AND CORA GORDON: "Food, Food" reprinted from *Three Lands on Three Wheels,* William Morrow & Co., © 1943, by permission of the publisher. Illustration by Jan Gordon reprinted from *On a Paris Roundabout,* The Bodley Head, © 1927, by permission of the publisher. HALDANE: Reproduced by permission of *Punch.* RENE JUTA: Reprinted from *Concerning Corsica,* by René Juta, with illustrations by Jan Juta, The Bodley Head Ltd. and Alfred A. Knopf, © 1926, by permission of Jan Juta. EMILY KIMBROUGH: Reprinted from *Floating Island,* Harper & Row, © 1968, by permission of the author. TIBOR KOEVES: From *Timetable for Tramps: A European Testament,* by Tibor Koeves. Copyright 1939 by Tibor Koeves. Copyright © renewed 1967 by Tibor Koeves. Reprinted by permission of Houghton Mifflin Company. RING LARDNER: Excerpted from *What of It?* Copyright 1925 Charles Scribner's Sons; copyright renewed 1953 Ellis A. Lardner. Reprinted with the permission of Charles Scribner's Sons, an imprint of Macmillan Publishing Co. STEPHEN LEACOCK: "Travel Is So Broadening" reprinted by permission of Dodd, Mead & Company, Inc., from *The Iron Man and the Tin Woman,* by Stephen